COUNTERTRANSFERENCE IN PSYCHOANALYTIC PSYCHOTHERAPY WITH CHILDREN AND ADOLESCENTS

The EFPP Clinical Monograph Series

Editor-in-Chief: *John Tsiantis*

Countertransference
in Psychoanalytic Psychotherapy
with Children and Adolescents

edited by

John Tsiantis
Senior Editor

Anne-Marie Sandler

Dimitris Anastasopoulos

Brian Martindale

published by

INTERNATIONAL UNIVERSITIES PRESS, INC.
Madison   Connecticut

for

The European Federation
for Psychoanalytic Psychotherapy
in the Public Health Services

First published in 1996 by
H. Karnac (Books) Ltd.
58 Gloucester Road
London SW7 4QY

Library of Congress Cataloging-in-Publication Data

Countertransference in psychoanalytic psychotherapy with children and
    adolescents / edited by John Tsiantis, senior editor, Anne-Marie
    Sandler, Dimitris Anastasopoulos, Brian Martindale.
        p.   cm. — (The EFPP clinical monograph series)
    "Published . . . for the European Federation for Psychoanalytic
    Psychotherapy in the Public Health Services."
    Includes bibliographical references and index.
    ISBN 0-8236-1084-5
    1. Countertransference (Psychology)   2. Child psychotherapy.
    3. Adolescent psychotherapy.   I. Tsiantis, J. (John)   II. European
    Federation for Psychoanalytic Psychotherapy in the Public Health
    Services.   III. Series.
    [DNLM: 1. Countertransference (Psychology)   2. Psychoanalytic
    Therapy—in infancy & childhood.   3. Psychoanalytic Therapy—in
    adolescence.   WM 62 C8552 1996]
    RJ505.C68C67   1996
    618.92'8917—dc20
    DNLM/DLC
    for Library of Congress   96-28231
                                                                      CIP

Manufactured in the United States of America

ACKNOWLEDGEMENTS

I wish to acknowledge the help and great encouragement that I received from Mr Cesare Sacerdoti of Karnac Books and from the Executive of the EFPP, especially my colleagues in the child section: Lydia Tischler, Birgit Hallerfors, and Miranda Feuchtwang. I also wish to express my gratitude to the editorial committee and in particular to Dr Brian Martindale, the EFPP Chairman, who has put a great deal of work into the final stages of the preparation of this Monograph.

My special thanks are also due to the contributors to this volume. I also wish to express my thanks to Mrs Mary Kritikou and Miss Magda Tammam for their secretarial assistance during the Monograph's preparation and to Elizabeth Holder and David Alcorn for the translation work. Finally, I wish to express my thanks to Eric and Klara King for the styling and editing of the book.

John Tsiantis
Athens, April 1996

ABOUT THE AUTHORS

ANNE ALVAREZ is Consultant Child Psychotherapist at the Tavistock Clinic, where she co-convenes the autism workshop; she is also Tutor to the Child Psychotherapy Training in the Department of Child Psychiatry, Turin University, and consultant at the Anna Freud Centre on Atypical Children. Among her many publications is the book *Live Company: Psychotherapy with Autistic, Borderline, Deprived and Abused Children.*

DIMITRIS ANASTASOPOULOS, MD, is an adult and child psychiatrist working in Athens. He was trained in adolescent psychiatry and psychotherapy at the Tavistock Clinic, London, and he is a training psychotherapist for adult and adolescent psychotherapists in Greece. He is a member of the Executive Committee of the Hellenic Association of Child and Adolescent Psychoanalytic Psychotherapy (H.A.C.A.P.P.).

JACQUELINE GODFRIND is a psychologist. She is a Full Member and a past President of the Belgian Psychoanalytical Society. She is especially interested in the theory of psychoanalytic technique and has written a book, *Les deux courants du transfert.*

ALEX HOLDER trained as a child and adult psychoanalyst in London at the Anna Freud Centre and the British Psychoanalytical Society. He was a staff member of the former for eighteen years before he moved to Hamburg in 1983, where he has since been head of the Department for Analytic Child and Adolescent Psychotherapy at the Michael-Balint-Institute. He is a member of the German and British Psychoanalytical Associations and is a training analyst.

DIDIER HOUZEL, MD, is currently Professor of Child and Adolescent Psychiatry at the University of Caen (France). He is a Full Member of the French Psychoanalytic Association. He has worked with Kleinian analysts, especially James Gammill in Paris and Donald Meltzer and the late Frances Tustin in England. He has published papers on "Psychic Envelopes" with Didier Anzieu, and other papers on the psychoanalytic approach to autism and childhood psychoses.

FRANÇOIS LADAME is a Psychiatrist and Psychoanalyst and currently President of the Swiss Psychoanalytical Society and Secretary of the European Association for Adolescent Psychoanalysis. He is Associate Professor at the University of Geneva School of Medicine and Chief of the Adolescent Consultation Centre, Service médicino-pédagogique, and co-editor of the journal *Adolescence* [Paris].

BRIAN MARTINDALE, MRCP, MRCPsych, is a Consultant Psychiatrist in Psychotherapy in London, having trained at the Maudsley and Cassel Hospitals. He is an Associate Member of the British Psycho-Analytic Society. He is Chairman and founding member of the European Federation for Psychoanalytic Psychotherapy.

ANNE-MARIE SANDLER is Director of the Anna Freud Centre in London (formerly the Hampstead Child Therapy Clinic). She is Past President of the British Psycho-Analytic Society and Vice-President of the International Psychoanalytical Association. She is a training analyst and is in practice with both adults and children and teaches in many countries.

JUDITH TROWELL, FRCPsych, is a Consultant Child and Adolescent Psychiatrist in the Child and Family Department of the Tavistock

Clinic in London. She is a Full Member of the British Psycho-Analytic Society and a Child Psychoanalyst.

JOHN TSIANTIS, MD, DPM, FRCPsych, is a psychiatrist, psycho-therapist, and child psychiatrist. He is currently Professor of Child Psychiatry at Athens University and Director of the Department of Psychological Paediatrics at the "Aghia Sophia" Children's Hospital in Athens. He is Chairman of the European Federation for Psychoanalytic Psychotherapy, and Chairman and Founding Member of the Hellenic Association of Child and Adolescent Psychotherapy. He is a member of the Editorial Advisory Board for *Journal of Child Psychotherapy, European Child and Adolescent Psychiatry,* and *British Journal of Psychiatry* (corresponding editor, Greece).

CONTENTS

FOREWORD TO THE SERIES

Brian Martindale

The European Federation for Psychoanalytic Psycho-therapy in the Public Health Services (EFPP) was founded in 1991 with a number of linked objectives. At their heart was and is a determination that knowledge and treatment skills stemming from psychoanalysis should become much more widely available and applicable to the general public with mental health problems who come for help from the "caring" professions.

In its short history, the EFPP has already made a considerable impact. Many of its member countries have been considerably assisted by the training standards for practitioners in psycho-analytic psychotherapy to which the EFPP aspires. The EFPP is organized into three sections: for individual adult psychoanalytic therapy, for child and adolescent psychoanalytic psychotherapy, for group psychoanalytic psychotherapy. Recognition of these three vital focuses of applied psychoanalysis through structural representation in the EFPP has created a unique spirit of co-operation between the sections.

The EFPP has already had four highly successful conferences which have been supported by delegates from many countries. The conferences have confirmed the large number of professionals who feel a need for an organization that supports local efforts to provide skilled psychodynamic understanding and therapy to mental health problems in these times of rapidly changing health-care philosophies. There is considerable public clamour for less technical approaches to these problems, yet in the cry for psychological understanding and help to face mental pain the public is vulnerable to superficial approaches, often those transiently in vogue. The EFPP hopes to counteract this by actively supporting the further development and spread of solidly founded psychoanalytic psychotherapy approaches and psycho-therapeutic centres.

Of course, books also assist the spread of knowledge, and their study will stimulate fresh thinking. It was with this in mind that we decided to start this series of EFPP monographs on clinical topics highly relevant to our crafts. We are grateful to Karnac books and Mr Sacerdoti for cooperation in this joint enterprise.

This volume, our first in the EFPP monograph series, is largely the outcome of the industry of the Editor-in-Chief of the Series and Senior Editor of this volume, Professor John Tsiantis. John is an excellent role model for those interested in developing psychoanalytic psychotherapy services in Europe. Amongst his many achievements are those stemming from his political skills and knowledge of the European Union, which have led to EU sponsorship in the setting up of the first training in child and adolescent psychoanalytic psychotherapy in Greece.

So we start our monograph series with this compilation of contributions from authors from several different European countries on a theme that lies at the heart of child and adoles-cent psychoanalytic psychotherapy—*countertransference* in the psychoanalytic psychotherapy of children and adolescents. We trust that the chapters highlight some of the many perspectives from which this topic needs to be viewed.

Chairman, EFPP
April 1996

INTRODUCTION

John Tsiantis

The chapters in this monograph constitute a wide-ranging investigation into the phenomenon of countertransference as it appears in the psychoanalytic psychotherapy of children and adolescents. The authors tackle the subject by bringing to it both their knowledge of various theoretical perspectives and their clinical experience and by demonstrating the crucial importance of countertransference in a wide range of clinical conditions and treatment settings.

Though countertransference is the main focus of the monograph, it is inevitable that transference is also considered. Indeed, it is widely accepted that, in clinical work, the core of the process in psychoanalytic psychotherapy and psychoanalysis is the transference–countertransference interaction, and it is therefore inevitable that the thoughts and viewpoints expressed should involve both concepts. This is particularly true if we accept that any therapeutic situation can be partly defined by the specific transference–countertransference space it generates.

All the contributors to the book are from member countries of the European Federation for Psychoanalytic Psychotherapy in the Public Health Services, and this has provided scope for colleagues from different parts of Europe to put forward their various viewpoints. However, the differences that are present in the clinical practice and the technique of psychoanalytic psychotherapy and psychoanalysis are based on a unified body of psychoanalytic thought. Another of the distinguishing marks of this monograph is its acceptance of the general principle that countertransference is a ubiquitous factor in child and adolescent psychoanalytic psychotherapy and psychoanalysis. It follows, therefore, that during therapy with children and adolescents, the recognition of countertransference, followed by unravelling and understanding the contributing factors from the patient and the therapist, and finally appropriate management and interpretation, are essential to effective treatment. Moreover, at the present time, in particular, when psychoanalytic psychotherapy and psychoanalysis (especially in the public sector and in particular in work with children and adolescents) is being scrutinized and investigated by governments, third-party insurance schemes, and researchers, it is important that we, the professionals who practice psychoanalytically informed therapies, should try to develop research methodologies in order to be able to monitor and evaluate the efficacy of our work.

The first chapter presents a selected review of the whole concept of countertransference and its historical development. This is followed by a review of the concept as it applies in the psychoanalytic psychotherapy of children and adolescents. It is suggested that in these particular situations there are three sources to the various factors that tend to interact with each other and elicit countertransference phenomena. These three sources are:

1. the child or adolescent in therapy;
2. the parents and family of the child;
3. the therapist.

The most important contributions in the literature concerning these sources are then discussed and reviewed in considerable detail.

In chapter two, Judith Trowell explains the importance of baby and infant observation (as developed by Esther Bick) during the training of colleagues to be psychoanalytic psychotherapists of children and adolescents. This observation training has grown and developed, and it is a part of most psychoanalytically based therapy trainings and, in particular, of child therapy training. The author argues that observation affords trainees considerable scope for understanding the phenomena of countertransference, precisely because the observation setting is an ideal one for the development of countertransference reactions.

Trowell describes the value of observation by presenting material both from baby and infant observation as used in the training and also from the observation of diagnostic and therapeutic interviews. She connects this with the value of observation of one's own self in gaining the understanding of countertransference phenomena, which will ultimately allow the child psychotherapist and/or analyst to integrate information coming from the patient (conscious or unconscious) and information from within the therapist in diagnostic and therapeutic work.

In chapter three, Alex Holder reports that in psychoanalytic treatment there seems to be a special relationship between the frequency of sessions and the intensity and extent of transference phenomena and countertransference reactions. He also notes that the frequency of the sessions influences the characteristics of the psychoanalytic process that develops during therapy, especially the depth of therapy.

Holder investigates these points by presenting clinical work with a variety of cases, contrasting those in which the sessions were frequent with those when they were less frequent. He points out that it is not only the children who need time to bring out their unconscious wishes and fantasies; therapists, too, need time to get in tune and in touch, via their empathy and countertransference, with the child's unconscious inner world.

Holder also ascribes a somewhat wider meaning to the notion of countertransference, not seeing it as limited only to the therapist's immediate reactions to the child's material during the course of a session. In other words, he extends the notion of countertransference to cover the unconscious working-out process that takes place in the therapist between sessions, a process that may influence the overall attitude that the therapist may bring to bear upon the particular patient at the next session.

It is thus particularly important in less intensive therapy that therapists should observe, monitor, and scrutinize their own inner emotional climate towards the patient before or at the beginning of the next session.

Holder refers to the psychoanalytic process, which he defines as one that evolves in the intermediate space between analyst/therapist and patient—something to which they both contribute. The contribution of the patient is to unravel his transference phenomena, while the therapist contributes through her understanding of countertransference reactions and phenomena, stemming from the patient's material, and by interpretative activity.*

In chapter four, Anne-Marie Sandler presents three case studies as the basis for a discussion of some problems of transference and countertransference that tend to emerge during child and adolescent analysis. The first case study reveals, inter alia, the extent to which countertransference reactions can contribute to an understanding of aspects of the child's inner world as it has taken shape through the relationship with the parents. These aspects include the projection by the parents onto the child of unwanted aspects of themselves. Sandler, too, notes that countertransference reactions on the part of the therapist are not confined to the duration of the session but, as Holder has already observed, also occur before and after sessions.

Sandler uses her understanding of the transference and countertransference phenomena from all three case studies as the starting-point for a discussion of the difficulty that can emerge in the analysis of children and adolescents in establishing a treatment alliance with the analyst/therapist, which can prevent any progress at all being made in the treatment of the child or adolescent concerned. Sandler argues that this difficulty in establishing the treatment alliance can be seen in the attitude of the child towards therapy, which reflects a transference from the relationship with the primary object to the person of the

---

*For simplicity, in general discussions we have used feminine pronouns for therapists and masculine pronouns for patients.

therapist. This transference is described as so immediate and concrete that there is no room for elaboration, no capacity in the child to think or allow his self to regress and become close to another person because of an overwhelming fear of disappointment. Difficulties such as this are indicative of acute problems in the early relationship between the child and the primary object. On the other hand, the countertransference feelings of the therapist, who feels frustrated and denigrated, seem to reflect how hopeless, valueless, and unwanted the child or adolescent feels. Here again, an understanding of the countertransference phenomena helps the process of working through the patient's material and the difficulties that occur in the therapy of children and adolescents.

In chapter five, François Ladame deals with the concepts of transference and countertransference on the basis of Freud's original writings and subsequent developments in psychoanalytical thought and practice in connection with adult patients. He then moves on to an explanation of his own position through a presentation of clinical material drawn from therapeutic work with adolescents. More specifically, Ladame is postulating that the origin of transference can be seen as occurring in the actual offer of analysis, which is a reopening of the movement of closure that presided over the constitution of the individual. Ladame is suggesting that the establishment of transference reopens the earliest relationship, when the other was primal to oneself. He also notes that while countertransference was not initially accorded the necessary attention, it was later overemphasized in clinical practice as the unique tool for the dynamics of cure. Ladame discusses the pitfalls of this situation and draws attention to the significance of other important parameters in psychoanalytic practice. He then refers to certain developmental features of adolescence, together with certain forms of pathology that give a special colouring to transference and countertransference. This chapter describes the impact that these factors may have on the therapeutic relationship between the analyst and the child or adolescent in analysis.

In chapter six, Jacqueline Godfrind describes the countertransference feelings aroused in the child psychotherapist by the parents of her patients. She distinguishes two main functions of

the child psychotherapist: the interpreting one and the symbolizing one. She further develops the concept of "symbolizing
countertransference", considering it as the child psychotherapist's ability to think, give meaning, and communicate to her
patient—by linking psychically to his session material—transference feelings and experiences. She also considers the setting
as a third element in the therapeutic relationship, which permits
a psychic working through to occur and which can be seriously
affected by the presence of the parents, who can act as a
de-symbolizing agent. The author argues that the child psychotherapist's function can be greatly influenced by the parents'
actual or mental presence, which adds a new, complex intersubjective and environmental dimension in the therapeutic
relationship and may lead to distortions in the symbolizing qualities of the psychotherapist, affecting her understanding of the
child's fantasies and inner world.

In chapter seven, Anne Alvarez deals with countertransference in
therapy with neurotics, borderline patients, and psychotics. She
believes that the manner in which the therapist works through
her countertransference is an important consideration; in other
words, it is not enough that the therapist should pay attention to
the feelings that develop inside her and how these originated in
the patient. She should also devote attention to the way in which
these countertransference feelings are contained and trans-
formed, since this, ultimately, will have an effect on the shape
taken by her interpretations. Alvarez suggests that therapists
should hypothesize about the impact of their countertransfer-
ence-based interpretations on the patient before interpreting. In
other words, they should also use the countertransference feelings to try to anticipate their patient's likely reactions to the
interpretation. This will lead them to consider the perspective or
acceptable distance from which the interpretation is made.
Alvarez illustrates this through four short clinical vignettes: a
neurotic girl, a handicapped girl, an autistic boy, and a borderline schizoid girl.

In chapter eight, Didier Houzel describes the concept of the
psychic envelope, consisting of one maternal and one paternal
side, components that according to him—and other authors—are

of fundamental importance in developing the child's identity and sense of reality.

Houzel then goes on to note that the setting for therapy (and, more generally, the therapeutic situation) in work with psychotic children is of such a nature as to require a special understanding of the problems of transference and countertransference which emerge. He uses case studies to argue that psychotic children split off the maternal and paternal aspects of the combined object at a very primitive level. Houzel believes that therapists should first recognize these phenomena which develop in transference in order to proceed to work through the material. It is also important that therapists should understand these maternal and paternal aspects and properly reintegrate them in their own countertransference. He goes on to work out this innovative idea a little further, linking it with the concepts of the psychic envelope of bisexuality and of the therapeutic setting. He concludes by proposing that in therapy with psychotic children, there are certain special features that the setting and the more general therapeutic situation should possess: flexibility to allow the child's projection to be contained and understood by the psychotherapist's mind (a capacity that seems to belong to the maternal part), and firmness (which would appear to belong to the paternal part and function of the object).

The final chapter discusses issues that pertain to the transference and countertransference phenomena observed in the in-patient psychotherapy of traumatized children and adolescents. It is suggested that in-patient units for children or adolescents provide fertile ground for the development of a multiplicity of reactions of transference and countertransference, especially in the cases of psychologically traumatized children or adolescents. The phenomena of transference are directed towards the institution, the staff, and the therapist. It is also suggested that it is inherent in the functioning and nature of the therapeutic structure that a degree of splitting—"good therapist", "bad staff"—will occur. On the other hand, the staff—including the therapist— may develop strong countertransference reactions and may act on the basis of their feelings. This may lead to an impasse where the child or adolescent, the staff and the therapist, repeat the child's or adolescent's past. The chapter discusses means of providing a holding environment for the child or the adolescent during his in-patient treatment and for giving his therapist the space and the scope to explore the conflicts, difficulties, fears, and expectations.

* * *

This monograph is an addition to the previously modest literature available on countertransference in the psychoanalytic psychotherapy and psychoanalysis of children and adolescents. We hope it will prove useful to clinicians in the field and for the training and supervision of students in child and adolescent analysis and psychoanalytic psychotherapy.

Editor-in-Chief
April 1996

Countertransference
in Psychoanalytic Psychotherapy with Children and Adolescents

Countertransference issues in psychoanalytic psychotherapy with children and adolescents: a brief review

Dimitris Anastasopoulos & John Tsiantis

The development of the concept of countertransference

The aim of this chapter is to present a selected review of the concept of countertransference and to follow its historical development, giving an overview of counter-transference phenomena as it applies to psychotherapy with children and adolescents.

The first reference to countertransference comes in 1910, in a short essay by Freud entitled "The Future Prospects of Psycho-Analytic Therapy" (1910d). Freud returns to the subject in the 1915 publication "Observations on Transference-Love" (1915a) in which he refers specifically only to erotic countertransference reactions. In both articles, Freud describes countertransference as an obstacle to psychoanalytic treatment and a "result of the patient's influence on his [the therapist's] unconscious feelings" (1910d, p. 144). It has been suggested (Brandell, 1992) that it was his work with hysterics and the Dora case (Freud, 1905e) (which included powerful erotic transference components) that led him to identify erotic countertransference as a significant hindrance to the psychoanalytic process. Unfortunately, Freud never published an article specifically on countertransference.

Much has been written since Freud's time to develop and expand our understanding of countertransference phenomena. It was a significant development for psychoanalytic literature when countertransference began to be seen as a phenomenon of importance in helping the analyst to understand the patient. It was Paula Heimann who introduced the positive value of countertransference. Heimann (1950) describes it as "an instrument of research into the patient's unconscious" (p. 81), concluding that the therapist's countertransference is a "creation" of the patient, "a part of [his] personality" (p. 83).

Heinrich Racker (1968, pp. 134–135) has made a powerful contribution to the literature. In his well-known book, *Transference and Countertransference*, Racker accepts that countertransference phenomena are ubiquitous and that all the therapist's emotional reactions to the patient are born of countertransference, in analogy to the patient's transference.

Racker distinguishes two kinds of countertransference: direct countertransference, which occurs as a response to the patient's transference, and indirect countertransference, which is a response to any important figure outside the analytic situation (supervisors, colleagues, the patient's relatives or friends, and anyone else whose good opinion may be of interest to the therapist (Racker, 1968, p. 136). Racker further expanded his views to suggest that countertransference consists of two processes:

1. *Concordant or homologous identification*: in this type of countertransference, the therapist "identifies each part of her personality with the corresponding psychological part in the patient" (Racker, 1968, p. 134). Such countertransference is based on introjection and projection and is more or less the same as what others have called empathy.

2. *Complementary identification*, which is an "identification of the analyst's ego with the patient's internal objects". It is "produced by the fact that the patient treats the analyst as an internal (projected) object, and in consequence the analyst feels treated as such; that is, he identifies himself with this object" (Racker, 1968, p. 135).

Racker thinks of countertransference as both the greatest danger to psychoanalytic work and as an important tool for understanding the patient during it. He also makes a distinction between the countertransference position, when the therapist is experiencing the feelings and attitudes without acting or intervening, and the countertransference response, when the therapist's tolerance has been overcome by feelings that are acted upon, leading to intervention.

A notable contribution was made to the debate by Winnicott in his paper "Hate in the Counter-Transference" (1947). Winnicott suggests that countertransference should be seen as a therapeutically useful source of information about the intersubjective field and as a significant instrument for understanding aspects of the patient's personality. He, too, describes two kinds of countertransference: one that is a pathological response on the part of the therapist (close to the traditional view), and another that is referred to as "objective countertransference" and described as "the analyst's love and hate in reaction to the actual personality and behaviour of the patient" (p. 194).

Little (1951) pointed out that not only do the analyst's feelings mirror the patient's feelings, but also the patient's feelings mirror the analyst's feelings and he often becomes aware of real feelings in the analyst before the analyst becomes aware of them. Little proposed the rather extreme view that the therapist should reveal her countertransference feelings to the patient.

Little (1951), Kohut (1971), and Shane (1980) have also contributed to the "totalistic" view of countertransference. According to them, the universal (totalistic) view of countertransference, which was epitomized in Kernberg's article of 1965, sees countertransference as the total response of the child analyst to the patient, the parents, and the therapeutic situation. The analyst's reaction reflects her characerological structure and personality traits (both healthy and conflictual) in response to the specific and general behaviour of the patient. It also includes reactions stemming from culturally determined attitudes, together with unintegrated identification(s) and unresolved transference issues towards the training analyst or other important persons in the therapist's life.

Giovacchini (1981) has also made an important contribution to the field of countertransference, especially where countertransference problems in therapy with adolescents and severely disturbed adults are concerned. Although he emphasizes that unrecognized countertransference can have a deleterious impact upon treatment, he notes that countertransference is ubiquitous and to be found in every analytic interaction.

Giovacchini distinguishes two varieties of countertransference:

1. *The homogeneous*, which he sees as a rather predictable reaction due mainly to the patient's psychopathology and attitudes and which would cause more or less the same reactions in most therapists.

2. *The idiosyncratic*, which is a reaction arising from the unique qualities of the therapist's personal history and make-up (Giovacchini, 1985, p. 449).

Alvarez distinguishes between countertransference and what she calls "empathic perception" (Alvarez, 1983). In her article in this volume (chapter seven), she uses a narrow definition of countertransference, arguing that it includes "only the feelings aroused or evoked in the therapist by the patient" and not "a perception of something going on in the patient, which is un-accompanied by a similar or related feeling in the therapist"; the latter is what she calls an empathic perception. She believes that these perceptions are also useful for picking up previously unrecognized elements of the patient, but they are not counter-transference.

In the traditional definition, what we might call "counter-transference proper" includes the analyst's unconscious reaction towards the patient's transference, which is quite specific and originates in unresolved conflicts that complement those of the patient. The difference between the classic and the totalistic approaches to countertransference are discussed in detail by Brandell in his book *Countertransference in Psychotherapy with Children and Adolescents*, in which he gives a comprehensive review of the literature. He tabulates authors as being of Total-istic, Classicist, or Other orientation according to their theoret-ical conception or definition of countertransference (Brandell, 1992).

The definition of countertransference given by most authors, however, approximates to that of Epstein and Feiner (1983): that is, they see it as the therapist's contribution to the therapeutic situation. It is an inevitable, normal, and natural interpersonal event, involving a therapist who is a genuine co-participant in an ongoing process. Countertransference is thus a more-or-less direct reaction to the patient's transference. Marshall (1983) has proposed a categorization of countertransference reactions according to whether they are conscious or unconscious and whether they derive from the patient's particular make-up and psychopathology or come from the unresolved conflicts and particular background of the therapist. We should also mention Joseph Sandler's view of "countertransference and role responsiveness". The patient, he argues, brings into the therapeutic relationship infantile role relationships that he seeks to express or enact, as well as the defensive role relationships that he may have constructed and may wish to impose upon the analyst, thus experiencing the role relationship as a vehicle for gratification. Sandler's view is that the analyst's "role responsiveness" shows itself not only in her thoughts and feelings but also in her overt attitudes and behaviour, as a crucial element in what he calls the therapist's "useful" countertransference (Sandler, 1987). Others, such as Fliess (1953), Glover (1955), and Reich (1966), would define as countertransference any irrational response on the part of the therapist, and not only those stimulated by transference.

Finally, Brandell (1992, p. 2) points out that "differences in the experience of countertransference are more often associated with such factors as the patient's and the therapist's personalities and the unique quality of the intersubjective discourse that develops in a particular treatment situation" than with which of the two treatment methods is used (i.e. child psychotherapy or child psychoanalysis). We share that view, and this brief review of countertransference in child and adolescent psychotherapy thus makes reference to both therapeutic modalities. Anyway, it is useful to have in mind that countertransference phenomena can have a powerful effect on psychotherapy either as a useful therapeutic tool in one's work with patients, or as a hindrance with negative influence if the therapist is not aware of the origin of her own feelings.

Countertransference
and projective identification

We believe it would be useful to explore briefly the relationship between projective identification and the concept of counter-transference.

Projective identification ought probably to be seen as an evolving psychoanalytic concept on this subject, and one that only in recent years has come to be accepted by an increasing number of analysts and psychotherapists, regardless of their school. An explanation of the theoretical differences and different view points goes beyond the scope of this chapter but can be found in Joseph Sandler's comprehensive study, *Projection, Identification, Projective Identification* (1988).

Melanie Klein (1946) connected projective identification with the process of development and also with the distortion of the analyst's image in the fantasies of the patient, though not—directly—with countertransference, which she saw as an obstacle to analysis (Klein, 1957).

Heimann gave projective identification a central and unique role in the development of countertransference phenomena, stating that in her opinion countertransference was "created by the patient" and contained "part of his personality" (Heimann, 1950, p. 83).

Racker linked the countertransference reactions on the part of the therapist to the mechanism of projective identification in the patient, arguing that it led to the analyst's identification with the self or object representation with which the patient, too, identified her in the projection. As we have already seen, this allowed him to distinguish between concordant countertransference and complementary countertransference (Racker, 1968).

The interaction and cross-influence model of Bion (1962, 1963), which used the concepts of the container (which receives projection) and the contained (what is projected by the subject onto the object) is, of course, based on the mechanisms of projective identification, which it links directly to countertransference.

Rosenfeld is among the authors who have written extensively on the role played by projective identification in countertransference in work with schizophrenic, psychotic, and borderline patients (Rosenfeld, 1987). More specifically, Rosenfeld states: "Not only does it affect the aspects of the self which are moved about but the object under the influence of projective identification is strongly affected by it"; and a little further on: "Projective identification can include transformations of the self, and the object, leading to confusion, depersonalization, emptiness, weakness and vulnerability to influence which goes so far as being hypnotised or even put to sleep" (p. 170).

Joseph (1988) points out that although projective identification is a fantasy, it has a strong effect on its receptor. If the analyst is open and capable of recognizing what she is experiencing, it can be a very powerful method of understanding the true wealth of the phenomena of countertransference. Joseph argues that by means of the mechanisms of projective identification the therapist can be brought to the point of adopting attitudes and feelings that do not belong to her but are parts that the patient has projected on to her.

Kernberg (1988) argues that projective identification is the predominant psychic mechanism which (as in the case of very regressed patients) can cause such intense countertransference reactions in the therapist that she has to work them through outside the therapeutic sessions in order to be able to understand them.

Grinberg (1979) elaborates the concept of projective counter-identification in countertransference as a mechanism for describing the analyst's reaction—or a significant part of it—that belongs to the intensity and unique quality of the patient's projective identification. He thus sees countertransference as stemming from activation of the neurotic parts of the analyst.

Grotstein accepts Grinberg's term "projective counter-identification" as a particular kind of countertransference. He argues that both projective identification and projective counter-identification are perceived by the analytical therapist as an "alteration in his state of mind while listening to the patient" (Grotstein, 1985, p. 200). He goes on to note that it is the therapist's ability to contain that will convert this experience into something meaningful for the patient and the therapeutic process.

Feldman (1992) reports that in many cases the therapist has to deal not only with fantasy projections onto the object, thus ascribing to it capacities that originate in the psychic state of the patient, but also an active and dynamic process in which the psychic state of the object is affected by the projections.

To conclude, countertransference can be seen—in accordance with the authors cited above and with others who agree with their position—as the therapist's reaction to the patient's projections into her. The reaction may stem either from the stimulation or awakening of immature neurotic parts of the therapist herself or from the creation or generation of feelings and fantasies that are wholly to be attributed to the intensity and quality of the patient's projective identification. Needless to say, the more emotionally open (and thus ready to accept projection) the therapist is, and the more regressed the patient is, the greater will be the likelihood of the formation of powerful countertransference reactions which can be used to understand the material during therapy. It would seem that both these conditions would also apply to psychotherapeutic work with children and adolescents.

Countertransference in child psychotherapy

One would have expected that in parallel with the development of countertransference theory and technique in therapy with adult patients, there also would have evolved delineation's of different kinds of countertransference emanating from the psychoanalytic psychotherapy of children. However, this was long delayed, and such themes have begun to appear in the literature only in recent years. Some possible explanations of this have been advanced, and the most important of them are described below.

First of all, there was a long delay in the general recognition and acceptance of transference neurosis in the analysis of children. Secondly, the absence of any concern about countertransference in the past may also have been a reflection of the special nature of the personality of child therapists, regardless of their pre-analytic background. The first child analysts were predominantly educators (Kohrman, Fineberg, Gelman, & Weiss, 1971), and they dealt with children from the lower socio-economic strata; adult therapists, however, work in the medical mode, in which there is a distinct distance between patient and therapist.

This gave rise to confusion in psychotherapeutic technique between the pedagogical and the psychotherapeutic type of intervention. Apart from its other differences from psychotherapy, the pedagogical intervention meant that the therapist became a parental surrogate, gratifying the needs of the child without maintaining a stance of analytic neutrality. In this context, Temeles (1967) notes that gift-giving in child psychotherapy was used at this time—in part, at least, because the children treated were deprived and in part because of social stereotypes about child-rearing. This approach reflected, inter alia, loyalties, identifications, and unresolved transference by the therapist to teachers, who were closely identified with these issues. The pedagogic attitude to child psychotherapy, stemming from tradition and theory, supports the acceptability of such counter-reactions. It is difficult to say which came first: the technique, the theory, the loyalty to and identification with the teacher, or a countertransference reaction that became justified or acted out and defended through the technical modification used subsequently.

Factors evoking
countertransference reactions

We now move on to a description of the factors that are the cause of countertransference reactions in child and adolescent psychotherapy and which may be triggered by the therapist herself, by the child, by the parents, or by the particular features of the therapeutic relationship.

Although countertransference always "comes" from the therapist, a countertransference response can be triggered by the psychopathology of the patient or some other element in the situation which is the result of a "fit" between patient and therapist. If the therapist's response is at least partially based on her early needs and is not solely the result of the influence of the patient, then we can talk about countertransference in the totalistic definitive. Clearly enough, most reactions include some component of countertransference (Schowalter, 1985). Furthermore, countertransference refers to both the influence of the past on the therapist's anxieties and feelings about the child or the parents and the influence that they have on the psychotherapist's feelings and associations. Even if countertransference feelings denote elements of the therapist's unresolved conflicts, they still express a response to the distress and most painful anxieties of the child or adolescent and to his personal experience and development. The anxiety experienced by the therapist as a result of countertransference is a form of participation in the patient's efforts to deal with self-threatening issues. Similarly, countertransference resistance in work with children and adolescents is an indication of the unwillingness of the therapist to identify personal sources of anxiety and connect them with the intrapsychic life and family transactions of the patient (McCarthy, 1989).

Countertransference also includes emotional reactions that stem from the parent's role in the development of the youngster's self, and they also reflect aspects of the child's inner world and the product of family dynamics (McCarthy, 1989). In general, therapists tend—up to a point—to be fond of their patients, since otherwise treatment would be either overwhelming or impossible. This makes them more perceptive of their patients' projections and, consequently, more apt to develop feelings of countertransference. Countertransference may include the feelings a therapist may have towards a patient, regardless of the origins of the feelings. According to Giovacchini (1974), countertransference reactions include many personal elements common to the character structure of many clinicians which produce fairly similar responses. The existence of countertransference should probably be seen as contributing to an understanding of the process of psychotherapy. On the other hand, empathic failures are part and parcel of the therapeutic process and should not be viewed as unusual or only as indicators of the psychopathology of therapist or patient. The treatment of difficult patients raises a number of narcissistic issues for every therapist. It requires the painful confession of unresolved issues—an admission that the therapist's professional competence is not as perfect as she would like to think it—and the recognition of resentment towards the patient as the agent who brought these realizations to the foreground (Palombo, 1985). On the other hand, Giovacchini (1974, p. 282) argues that transference–countertransference reactions, if properly handled, can become an event equivalent to the lifting of the "infantile amnesia" that prevents the recovery of infantile memories and traumatic childhood events. Baudry (1991) identifies the therapist's beliefs, attitudes, personal style, and characteristic reactions as crucial components in her therapeutic approach. Professional identity is another factor here. Baudry refers to the therapist's individual background, which may lead her to prefer work with some kinds of patients and makes her more prone to some emotional reactions than others.

Chessick (1992) describes the transference–countertransference reaction in terms of the importance of the cultural and family background and the infantile fantasies that provide each individual with a mental set determining the way in which that individual experiences the world, together with a non-verbal grounding that is fundamental for his or her activities, human relationships, and self-concept.

We believe that it is clear from our examination of the issue to this point that whatever approach is adopted to countertransference (totalistic, classical, or other), it could be said that countertransference is a phenomenon concerning the therapist as an individual: in her relationship with the patient, of course, but as an individual who participates with the whole background of her personality and character. On the other hand, when talking of therapy with young patients (and with infants and children in particular), we also have to consider the participation of the parents, who are present not only as specific objects but also as active participants in the life of the patient and the therapeutic process.

Against this background, countertransference reactions can develop in response to:

a. transference and/or projections of patients, their families, and/or their environments—such states are often particularly intense in psychotherapeutic work with very disturbed children and adolescents;
b. feelings in the therapist that stem from her own early experiences, unresolved psychic conflicts, or incompletely analysed neurotic areas that are triggered by the patient's states as in (a).

In most cases, strong countertransference reactions stem from a mixture of factors in both categories, but the setting itself, the age of the child or adolescent patient, and his tendency to regress easily can greatly increase the intensity and frequency of the development of countertransference reactions.

Thus, when we examine the factors that influence the particular nature of countertransference in the psychotherapy of children and adolescents, we have three categories of factors that interact with each other: those stemming (1) from the child or adolescent in therapy, (2) from the parents and family of the child, and (3) from the therapist herself.

Countertransference factors in relation to children

Communication in child psychotherapy is mainly on a non-verbal symbolic level, through play and action. It is common knowledge that children express themselves primarily through action rather than words. In psychotherapy, the use of play is one of the particular ways in which children communicate their feelings and fantasies, and the therapist uses it as she would use verbal communication. The child psychotherapist tries to develop her understanding through the use of symbols in play, through body postures and attitudes, and through mimicry, which are in direct contact with the more primitive parts of the child. There is thus less distance between the unconscious material of the child and the therapist, and this may contribute to the appearance of feelings of countertransference.

The therapist participates actively in the session and joins in the play activity. Often, the therapist's communications to the child stem from the feelings evoked in her by the child's non-verbal expressions. The therapist has to evaluate and decide constantly, under the pressure of invitations to act and of the child's primitive needs. There is often not enough time, boundaries are not clear-cut, and the therapist has to rely on her intuitive understanding of the situation. It is difficult for the therapist to weigh up the consequences of her action and thus develop countertransference feelings and thoughts. James Anthony (1986) expressed the view that countertransference phenomena are more likely to arise in work with children than with adults. He also suggested that although countertransference phenomena are more intense in the treatment of children, child psychotherapists are less prone to disruptive countertransference responses because the likelihood of induced countertransference is high and expected. Libidinal and aggressive drives that are expressed through actions by the children are common in child psychotherapeutic work and are more likely to provoke direct and personal reactions in the therapist than when expressed verbally as wishes and fantasies (Schowalter, 1985).

We also know that, among children, regression generally takes the form of action. The direct demand for response and action made by the child leads of its own accord to countertransference—that is, a regressive response—in the therapist (Kohrman et al., 1971). The child's expression of transference is direct and seemingly primitive, and his entire inclination is towards action rather than verbal association, thus prompting the therapist in the direction of regressive responses in her countertransference. Other factors to which attention has been drawn are:

> The fact that the child is nearer to its unconscious process than the adult, that the analyst is continuously involved in sequences of action leaving little time for reflection, and that meaningful content is expressed in symbols and through action. All the above factors have direct consequences for the degree of the analyst's exposure to countertransference. [Piene, Auestad, Lange, & Leira, 1983, p. 52]

In other words, it seems to be inherent in therapeutic work with children that the child's communications impose great demands on the therapist's contact with her own feelings and on her ability to comprehend the unconscious contact expressed and received. McCarthy (1989) suggests that analytic work with children and adolescents resurrects the analyst's anxieties and childhood feelings as a result of the twofold influence of the child's anxiety and the dialogue of the child's inner object. Alvarez (1983) puts forward the idea that the raw and primitive behaviour of younger children tends to evoke anxiety in the therapist which may stem from unresolved pre-genital conflicts. The child psychotherapist may even find herself acting out with bursts of unreasonable restraints or interpretations about fears of loss, as a countertransference reaction to a subtle provocation coming from the child. Alvarez (1983) and McCarthy (1989) have also suggested that the tendency of children and adolescents to act rather than thinking verbally, and their limited tolerance for highly ambivalent feelings, represent developmentally based sources for the reactions of transference and countertransference. It is as if the children and adolescents were constantly seeking to test the limits of the analyst's power and authority.

Another important factor to be considered is that the child's regression is not expressed and recognized as it is with adults; in a way, it is an additional regression. The child's communications are closer to the primary process and to unconscious material than those of many adults. As a consequence, there are less clearly defined boundaries between fantasies, wishes, and drives—which are more openly and directly expressed—and external reality. In work with children, the nature of the drives expressed in the particular transference relationship is open and direct, and the demands for drive gratification are so intense that they sometimes lead to the seduction of the therapist and an outright assault on her. The direct physical and emotional demands and the empathy required in the face of such direct requests may evoke countertransference reactions related to unconscious sibling rivalry and may revive other infantile needs in the therapist. We also know that feelings from the pre-verbal period of life tend to linger on, though they are probably inaccessible to language. As a result, the child psychotherapist is under the pressure to be responsive and receptive primarily to non-verbal communication and to rely heavily on her counter-reaction and countertransference feelings. Therapy thus comes to be based on countertransference more than is the case with adults, and communication and transaction during child psychotherapy are expressed on a pre-verbal level in which the defences used are largely primitive ones. The feelings of the psychotherapist form one of the best tools for understanding what is going on in the child, who expresses himself mainly through action and body language.

Therapists working with children who function on a pre-oedipal level have reported that these children tend to transfer (or project) split-off parts of the self into the psychotherapist.

This may result in a situation in which the psychotherapist experiences the emptiness, loneliness, worthlessness, uncontrollable rage, and so forth, projected onto her (Piene et al., 1983). Because of this massive projection, it is often difficult for the therapist to distinguish between what is transference and what is the patient's real life.

Similarly, the defences used by regressed children and adolescents—like those of very regressed adults—may cause the development of countertransference responses in the therapist that impede the therapeutic relationship. For example, the child psychotherapist may become the receptor of transference feelings and reactions that are sometimes so massive as to be difficult to cope with. Projective identification is used by some children and adolescents as the main tool for communicating and expressing needs, unbearable feelings, fragmented and disintegrated parts of themselves, and psychic traumas. It can then be very painful and difficult for the therapist to allow herself to be used as the container of these feelings while at the same time understanding what is being communicated. Quite frequently, these projections are defensive manoeuvres in which "bad" parts of the self are discharged onto the therapist, and are then followed by attempts to exert omnipotent control over her. On some occasions, one finds that the child is projecting onto the therapist the feelings of conflict that he or she has experienced with the parent of the opposite sex. The therapist, in turn, may feel sexually stimulated by the child's seductive behaviour. She may also misread the child's hunger for closeness and physical contact as seduction because of conflicts stemming from her own early childhood (Berlin, 1987). On this point, Piene et al. (1983) suggests that when young children feel free to touch the analyst, crawl into her lap, jump on her from heights, or kiss her, this can create intense reactions regardless of the child's sex. It is therefore important that the therapist try to delineate therapeutic boundaries with the child, without necessarily being distant or defensive. Another closely related fact is that the therapist, as the bearer of the child's feelings, usually cannot feel a sense of alienation from the patient. She invariably becomes the embodiment of the trauma the child has suffered and of the deficit that the child has. Ruptures in the therapeutic process will inevitably be experienced by the patient as injurious. The patient's rage will be mobilized towards the therapist and may call for "revenge", leading to acting-out reactions.

Some children often respond with a single word, or their play lacks imagination. Periods of silence or empty play are not unusual in psychotherapy with children. Some children are able to communicate only in a rudimentary or non-symbolic manner, while others seem able to express themselves but to be inhibited about doing so.

Sessions of this kind put a strain on the therapist, who may feel bored, frustrated, and useless. Although this is probably the only way in which the non-expressive child can tell his story, experiencing and tolerating such feelings somehow becomes equated with the difficulty of containing the amorphous quality of the countertransference stemming from the pre-mentational state of the regressed child (Geltner, 1987).

Countertransference responses may also be provoked by the demanding, stubborn, or hostile child, as well as by the passive, submissive child who is fearful of object loss and has an intense need of love. Symbiotic needs expressed symbolically in play or through insistence on physical contact for merging, demands for need fulfilment, and material related to the oral, anal, and phallic–oedipal phases are additional factors that can arouse unconscious issues in the therapist (Marcus, 1980). The angry, domineering child may elicit retaliatory anger rather than firmness and gentle clarification of what is or is not permitted. The withdrawn, needy child may elicit an inability to reach out and provide an understanding, empathic relationship encouraging exploration and play.

With severely disturbed children, an understanding of the developmental data that emerge during transference and countertransference may be crucial for the outcome of therapy. Most therapists, for example, find the child's masturbation during therapy time paralysing or observe that it elicits retaliatory feelings in them, touching on their own related—and possibly unresolved—conflicts of the past (Berlin, 1987). Palombo (1985) suggests that when psychotherapists attempt to treat hostile or neglected children, they appear to reach the absolute limits of their capacity for concordant responses. He further suggests that in work with deprived and severely disturbed children, the therapist's attention should be focused on the kind of event or intervention that caused the reaction, which may be related to her countertransference. It is also suggested that despite the therapist's best efforts to create the space for the repair and restoration of the relationship, this is often not possible with severely deprived and disturbed children, since their rage may be seen as an organizing experience that prevents further disintegration: if they give up their hatred, fragmentation will follow (Palombo, 1985).

To sum up, there are a series of factors that intensify and make the appearance of feelings of countertransference more likely in the psychotherapist during therapeutic work with children. These are: (a) the primitive, regressed material produced by children, whose psychic world is closer to that of the unconscious and primary processes, together with massive use of primitive psychic mechanisms; (b) developmental immaturity, which reduces tolerance to ambivalence and deprivation and leads to such direct expression of needs and demands to be gratified, or to the direct expression of feelings of hostility and rage, especially in the case of severely deprived children; and (c) the very nature of the therapeutic relationship, which often contains direct and physical contact with the children, whose limits are unclear, and which involves pre-verbal expression and communication with disturbed children who act and move rather than "talk". In these conditions, the therapist's feelings are of much greater significance for an understanding of the patient, and the therapist is much more open to feelings of countertransference.

All these factors may very easily trigger countertransference reactions, mobilizing the therapist's unresolved pre-genital conflicts and infantile needs.

Countertransference factors
in relation to adolescents

Adolescent psychopathology and psychotherapy have traditionally been the "step-children" of child psychopathology and psychotherapy, and an occasional area of challenge for adult psychotherapists. It is true that the fluctuating and often unexpected reactions of adolescents, their mood swings, and their challenging of the therapeutic and personal boundaries have—over time—brought many therapists to the point of working more with adults than with adolescents. There are also a number of factors that contribute to the development of various types of countertransference reaction in psychotherapeutic work with adolescents. Some of these factors will be mentioned below.

While adolescents share many of the features of children and some of those of adults, they also have characteristics of their own in their development and make-up which may make a particular contribution to the growth of countertransference. Adolescence is a stage of development in which elements from the previous, current, and subsequent phases are mingled. The course of each stage of therapy involves a variety of components. Feelings and the developmental levels of the transference alternate rapidly, and the overall course of therapy is sometimes swift and dramatic. The therapist is called upon to apply adaptability and flexibility in her approach to the adolescent patient, while remaining emotionally open to the adolescent's emotional swings. This, in conjunction with the massive use of projective identification, creates unusually powerful feelings of counter-transference, and the therapist's therapeutic role and neutrality are tested.

These factors combine to create a complex emotional situation with intense transference reactions in which the therapist must apply an approach of empathy and flexibility together with the insight needed to enable her to control her countertransference responses. It should be noted, however, that the time is not long gone since some therapists believed that the character structure and sense of identity of adolescents is too fluid and transitional to allow the development of transference and a stable therapeutic relationship, or that adolescents lacked the libido to make this possible. Other therapists thought that adolescents were too involved in the outer world, or too narcissistic, and they have also been described as "thinking in a concrete manner" or "not psychologically minded". Acting out, so often a feature of adolescence, has been cited as an obstacle to psychoanalytic psychotherapy. In the light of psychoanalytic developments regarding the treatment of severely disturbed and borderline cases, the question raised by Giovacchini (1974) was whether adolescents present us with a specific type of character pathology that is most likely to evoke particular forms of discomfort in the majority of therapists. It is generally assumed that some adolescents are difficult to treat because of their literal or concrete approach or because they are prone to acting out in motor behaviour or words. They can often be silent, remote, or hostile or can undermine the therapist. These patients project parts of the self, not discrete impulses. As a result, it is highly likely that the therapist will develop countertransference reactions. Alternatively, the adolescent's constant unwillingness to speak may lead to increasingly hostile demands for verbal material on the part of a therapist who feels deprived and narcissistically wounded by this. That, in turn, may lead to further acting out by the patient and the justification of the therapist's inability to cope with an "untreatable" youngster.

On the other hand, the cultural stereotypes that see adolescents only as vigorous rebels against society who seek the immediate gratification of their libidinal and aggressive impulses contain the image of the adolescent as a dangerous object with a vindictive stance towards adults, and such stereotypes may be at the root of the therapist's countertransference (Gartner, 1985; King, 1976). Adolescents often challenge our authority and professional competence. This may be developmentally sound, but it nonetheless causes considerable discomfort and countertransference feelings in the therapist. For example, a bright and highly competitive adolescent, who wishes to "defeat" the therapist at any cost, may create strong countertransference issues for the therapist (Berlin, 1987). One integral part of the formation of identity in adolescence is membership of a specific peer group, which allows the adolescent to define himself as separated from—and opposed to—other social and cultural groupings (Meissner, 1987, p. 482). Adolescents who are closely bound up with social and cultural processes often feel alienated and tend to oppose values and authority in order to preserve the integration of their own identity. Alienation is seen as a basic sense of loneliness, a feeling that one does not belong or is not a part of anything surrounding one, and it is connected with a sense of continuing frustration. The intensity of this can put an additional strain on the psychotherapist, who may take an authoritarian and didactic attitude (defending the values of the society to which she belongs) or may identify with the young, suffering victim of society, thus becoming unable to help him work through his despair.

Disturbed adolescents often use defences to counter their anxiety about physical and psychic change. Introspection and openness can still be threatening for adolescents if self-knowledge heightens conflicts about sexuality, dependency needs, or any aspect of individuation (McCarthy, 1989). Adolescents use a particular type of intellectualization—the asking of questions— which can become very intrusive for the therapist (Giovacchini, 1974). They also have a tendency towards sudden retreat, and sometimes display an inability to respect the rules and "rituals" of the psychotherapy setting, which, in their eyes, runs counter to the struggle for autonomy and their separation impulses. Psychic organization of this kind is capable of making the therapist feel guilty for having left the patient alone or imposed too many prohibitions. The therapist may then experience mounting depressive feelings as a result of increasing disappointment and aggression, and this can impede the therapeutic process (Wiesse & Kroczek-Weinstock, 1989).

In general, it could be said that the developmental phase of adolescence and the pathology that is sometimes characteristic of it can constitute fertile ground for the development of countertransference phenomena. For example, the adolescent's withdrawal from the childhood objects leads to a narcissistic over-cathexis of self. He becomes self-absorbed, self-centred, and self-concerned, sometimes going as far as narcissistic withdrawal and the disturbance of reality testing (Meissner, 1987, p. 479). Adolescents may also be fixated on childish goals and adaptive patterns and may be prevented from maturing by character pathology (Zaslow, 1985). The narcissistic regression often observed in adolescence leads to an intensification of narcissistic needs, and thence to the use of the mechanism of projective identification, employed in order to preserve the endangered integrity of the self. These reactions create a complex emotional situation with intense transference reactions that call for an empathic and flexible approach on the part of the psychotherapist, who should also possess the insight that will enable her to control her countertransference responses.

To put the matter briefly, the intense narcissism of adolescents and their rapidly-changing feelings and attitudes create particular difficulties for the therapist in containing them emotionally. Furthermore, the mingling of components from different developmental stages and the massive use of splitting and projective identification can lead to the development of intense feelings of countertransference. Adolescents often have a fragile relationship with reality and regress easily, while they also manifest an inclination towards acting and acting-out. If we add to this their tendency to challenge limits and authority and the development of intense feelings of transference with aggressive or sexual components, then we have a situation that tests the emotional make-up of the therapist and can often create feelings of countertransference.

Countertransference factors
stemming from parents and families

The therapeutic alliance involves the parents and child in combination. The younger the child, the greater the number of his activities that the parents should support, as auxiliary egos. As this relationship cannot be dealt with by means of interpretation, there are abundant opportunities for countertransference reactions. As McCarthy (1989) puts it, "Countertransference reactions clarify the meaning of those therapeutic interactions which recreate the child's experience in the family. They help in identifying the extent of the child's involvement in the family psychopathology, along with the significance of family processes in the child's maturation and use of unhealthy security operations."

The parents often feel rejected, principally because they over-idealize the therapist as the ideal parent. She is invested with the omnipotence and omniscience that the parents wish they had or that their own parents had had. They tend to over-comply with the limits of the therapist's authority, or, conversely, to test its limits. The therapist may respond inappropriately, failing to recognize the wounded narcissism of the parents and becoming entangled in her own countertransference feelings (Kohrman et al., 1971). Furthermore, the parents' defensive organization is challenged by the child's commitment to psychotherapy. As the child makes progress and develops autonomy, he challenges the parents' delusional self-image, revealing their use of primitive defences—that is, projective identification, idealization, and splitting (McCarthy, 1989).

The parents are often reluctant to support their child's psychotherapy by serving as an auxiliary ego whenever hostile transference elements appear in the relationship between the child and the therapist (Marcus, 1980). In other situations, the parents can be afraid of the exposure of their inadequacies and/or the family pathology. In such families, the parents distort the child's healthy trends and assign a neurotic meaning to the developmentally appropriate needs of their offspring (McCarthy, 1989). In these situations, parents quite often signal to the child and/or the carers that they will stop supporting the treatment and withdraw, unconsciously equating psychotherapy and change with the rejection and abandonment of the family's ideology. In such cases, the child or adolescent patient can become anxious, depressed, and sometimes hostile, tending to act out his conflicts and quite often refusing to attend sessions.

Countertransference gives the therapist some clues to the nature of the child's intrapsychic reality and to his experience in the family. The analysis of countertransference can be a useful tool for understanding the resistance of children and parents and for promoting an understanding of the role of the family in the psychopathology of the child and the impact of the child's developmental defects on the family (McCarthy, 1989). Both Heimann (1950) and Racker (1968) imply that there is a need to deal with all the emotional responses induced by the patient, the patient's transference, and the therapist's emotional history. Parents may unconsciously induce guilt in the child in therapy while remaining ambivalent about the child's progress. They fear the possible loss of the child as an aspect of their self or as a substitute parent: the maturing child is useful to the emotionally damaged parent, who uses him to lower his or her own anxiety and keep his or her psychic balance. Such parents tend to oppose the therapist's efforts, manipulating and violating the therapeutic contract. The child psychotherapist needs to resist her tendency to respond to such situations with anger or a threat to withdraw her interest from the case.

The mother's transference to the child's therapist may also be affected by the psychotherapist's gender, since she may find it difficult to "share" her child with another woman, who will be seen as an idealized or primitive mother. Feelings of inadequacy and jealousy may emerge, and she may feel herself in competition with the therapist for her child's loyalty (Tyson, 1980). It is quite common for the therapist—for reasons of her own—to become trapped in the mother's transference feelings and to react with countertransference by entering into competition with her. This may be the result of the therapist's own unresolved conflicts in connection with her parents.

Parents can also be intrusive, trying to manipulate the therapist as they manipulated the child, in response to the feeling of being threatened by the possibility that their defects and faults will be revealed: they will be narcissistically unable to sustain their own emotional balance.

The child psychotherapist has to deal with all these responses and also with the parents' projections, elaborating on her own feelings of countertransference and trying to keep the therapeutic space clear of such intrusion or interference. In some cases, the child psychotherapist has to deal with parents who are neglecting their children, are unable to respond emotionally to their needs, and generally mistreat them. This is not the easiest thing to deal with, as a therapist must find some way of liking her patients and may develop strong negative feelings towards such parents. This situation often develops in mother–infant dyadic psychotherapy (Gochman, 1992). In such cases, intense countertransference reactions stemming from the therapist's identification with the child may develop, causing the therapist to become aggressive towards the parents. This may be indirectly expressed during sessions with the child, who for his own reasons may foster the bad parent/good parent–therapist splitting.

The parents thus participate as third parties in the psychotherapy of children, and they have a direct or indirect impact on its course and the potential for its continuation. When they feel that they are narcissistically wounded and rejected or that their inadequacies are being revealed during psychotherapy, or that they are in danger of "losing" their child or the established status quo in their family, they will often react strongly. They may idealize or underestimate the therapist, refuse to support therapy, intervene in or interrupt the therapeutic process, attack the work being done by the therapist, or unconsciously cause guilt in the child. This creates an atmosphere in which it is easy for the therapist to develop countertransference reactions. The mother's transference towards the therapist may be particularly strong, with feelings of inadequacy, jealousy, or envy. Parents who are particularly neglectful or inadequate inevitably test the feelings of the therapist, who may easily adopt attitudes and take decisions influenced by her countertransference. On the other hand, if she is in a position to control her countertransference towards the parents, she can use it as a valuable tool in understanding the dynamics of the family and the possible involvement of the parents in the development of the child's psychopathology.

Zinner and Shapiro (1972) and Feinsilver (1985) note the role that projective identification plays in intensifying the phenomena of countertransference in therapeutic work with the parents and families of adolescents.

One way in which the therapist can cope with these issues—especially in cases of physical or sexual abuse and divorce—is to remain in touch with her own feelings and try to understand them. This process will help the therapist to keep the feelings at a distance, without being flooded with anxiety or becoming aggressive towards the parents, thus disturbing the therapist's ability to understand and interpret the material. The powerful countertransference phenomena that develop in such cases may also cause the therapist to experience intense anger and negative feelings; these feelings may flood her and lead her to adopt a defensive and highly distanced attitude, preventing her from being available to behave towards the parents in a manner that goes no further than criticism, or even causing him to avoid them altogether. The therapist may then rationalize this attitude under a cover of analytic neutrality (Garber, 1992).

Countertransference factors stemming from the therapist

In a very enlightening paper, Kohrman and his co-workers explore the countertransference problems of child analysts and psychotherapists (Kohrman et al., 1971). They refer to a panel on the indications and goals of child analysis (Bernstein, 1957) at which the problems were discussed. The issues presented in the panel were as follows: the personality of the therapist, who makes the decision regarding what type of treatment the child will have; the therapist's rescue fantasies and her reaction to the child's libidinal and aggressive fantasies; the taboo subject of sexual countertransference in child analysis; the overstimulation of the child's dependency needs. Another issue mentioned was the therapist's countertransference, which develops right from the very first contact. It was suggested that delays in the termination of treatment might also be the result of countertransference, and in particular of the envious countertransference of male therapists towards mothers. It was noted that the functioning of the child therapist as a real object during treatment can create countertransference problems such as difficulty in observing analytically when participating in the play of a pre-school child.

One factor that seems to be related to the development of countertransference problems is the motivation that led the individual to become a child and adolescent psychotherapist. It has been suggested that some colleagues become child therapists in order to prove that they are better mothers or fathers than their own parents (Schowalter, 1985). This sets up intense countertransference phenomena, since in effect what is happening is that the therapist is coming into contact with facets of her self that her parents ignored when she was a child. In such cases, positive parental countertransference from the therapist to the child develops.

In other cases, the therapist whose motivation in working with young patients was a reaction formation against underlying hostility may rationalize punitive behaviour towards her patients, or, out of a desire to prove herself a better parent, become excessively permissive and gratifying, finding it difficult to set limits (Hammer & Kaplan, 1967).

In still another set of instances, it may be that the motivation can be traced back to non-gratification of the therapist's own personal dependency needs. By choosing to work with emotionally deprived children and adolescents, the therapist gratifies a part of her own dependency needs. The result, however, is the development of countertransference reactions and phenomena that reinforce the dependence of the children and adolescents on therapy without any effective therapeutic progress being made.

Another possibility is that the therapist may have unresolved oedipal needs and desires, which could be summarized as a wish to be loved and needed. Because of their great emotional needs, emotionally mentally disturbed children tend to cling tightly to the therapist in the hope of gratifying—at whatever cost—their needs for care and affection.

A therapist who chooses to specialize in adolescent psychotherapy may have a psychic make-up that is highly dependent on the receipt of certain types of narcissistic gratification. We all know of the adolescent's ability to provoke powerful feelings of impotence, inadequacy, worthlessness, and doubt. It is thus easy for a therapist who is unconsciously expecting gratification as the object of admiration and identification for the adolescents to develop negative countertransference feelings towards her patients, rejecting them, or, alternatively, accusing herself of not being the ideal figure for them. The striving towards omnipotence is one central feature of those who choose to work with adolescents, and the adolescent's need for an ego ideal and his search for an identity may be very attractive factors in the therapist's choice (Malmquist, 1978). Many therapists find work with patients in early adolescence uncomfortable, feeling overwhelmed by the presence of so many different aspects of development and by the rapid fluctuation in the emotional growth of their patients (Gartner, 1985).

Another factor that is sometimes connected with the development of countertransference reactions is the image of the "substitute parent" which the child psychotherapists may have about themselves or which their colleagues may attribute to them. There is also a commonly held belief that child psychotherapists are, by definition, more maternal, more benevolent, and more in tune with child behaviour: more child-like. It has been suggested that they are closer to primary-process functions, or find it easier to gain access to them (Kohrman et al., 1971). It follows that even the attitudes of colleagues, based on these beliefs, may play some part in the development of countertransference feelings by child psychotherapists.

It has been suggested that the development of countertransference is more or less inherent in the personality structure and internal world of the child psychotherapist (Waksman, 1986). Waksman argues that in her work the child psychotherapist has to make reparation to at least two internal objects, and that consequently the development of countertransference is inevitable. One internal object represents the child part of the therapist herself, which has not been sufficiently repaired in personal analysis, while the other(s) represents the ideal parents of the therapist's early years, attacked in fantasy.

Child psychotherapists have to cope with their own infantile longings in addition to those projected onto them by their patients. When the child's conflicts, projections, or transference feelings touch on the therapist's unresolved infantile longings, she tends to defend herself by repressing those feelings. The therapist then becomes concerned with rules and setting the limits and may end up as excessively strict and rigid.

In a very comprehensive passage, Bick refers to the countertransference difficulties imposed on the therapist by the patient's projections:

> . . . the strain imposed on the mental apparatus of the analyst both by the content of the child's material and by its mode of expression. The intensity of the child's dependence, of his positive and negative transference, the primitive nature of his fantasies, tend to arouse the analyst's own unconscious anxieties. The violent and concrete projections of the child into the analyst may be difficult to contain. Also, the child's suffering tends to evoke the analyst's parental feelings. He may identify with the child against the parents, or with the parents against the child. [Bick, 1962, p. 330]

Connected with this is the ability that the therapist must have to identify herself with the child while at the same time maintaining her therapeutic stance and objective attitude towards the child—which is equivalent to her capacity for the establishment of empathy. However, the impact of the child's projections may affect the therapist's capacity to develop empathy, since the projections may be felt in a personal way by the psychotherapist who is herself immersed in the primitive content of the patient's early developmental phase (Giovacchini, 1974). Inevitably, then, the therapist will be caught up in countertransference reactions.

One common form of countertransference reaction is for the child psychotherapist to identify not only with the patient, but also with the child's parents, reacting towards them as if they were her own parents. This form of countertransference identification may be observed when the therapist subtly encourages an adolescent's rebellion against his parents or some other form of authority or when the therapist serves as the child's advocate against the parents in order to gratify her own personal needs. To do this, however, is to work against the benefits of therapy for the child.

There is a well-known "saviour complex" among child and adolescent psychotherapists. The social and psychological attitude towards the disturbed children as victims justifies the "rescue fantasies" of therapists. The therapists may identify with their patients, fantasizing that the care they are giving to the children is that which their true parents were never able to give them, thus making them the good, loving parents the children never had. It has also been noted that some child and adolescent psychotherapists feel more comfortable with younger people because of a failure to overcome their own early anxieties about strangers and other adults (Gartner, 1985). Such rescue fantasies may lead the therapist to identify with the ideal parental figure, bringing her to a belief in her own omnipotence and ability to eliminate the despair and hopelessness of severely disturbed and deprived children and adolescents and a refusal to accept failures or defeats. On the other hand, over-identification with the parental role may lead to disillusionment, anger, competition, and projection towards the child and his parents (Gartner, 1985). A therapist who has identified with the ideal parental figure cannot avoid tension in dealing with the patient's real parents. This often leads to feelings of guilt and to the inappropriate exclusion of the parents from the therapeutic process. Such therapists may also have problems in the termination phase of treatment.

Beiser (1971) found that therapists working with children—as opposed to those who worked with adults—tend to identify more closely with the mother's role. Some of them may create the fantasy of being a better mother. This can cause an overcautious therapeutic attitude, because of an excessive concern not to hurt the child's parents, or it can lead to a competitive attitude towards them (Schowalter, 1985). On the other hand, the therapist is often pushed into a parental role by the child, who will initially provide a sense of trust, confidence, and security which later serves to reinforce dependence and feelings of inferiority and unworthiness (Zaslow, 1985). Therapists may sometimes tend to prove themselves to be "superparents", or may adopt the attitude that the parents are always wrong and are completely responsible for the child's disturbance. A refusal to meet or in any way involve the parents and a therapist's reluctance to hear signs of transference by the parent of the opposite sex are indications of countertransference. The parents' persistent ambivalence about the child's emotional progress in treatment may also contribute to the therapist's countertransference (McCarthy, 1989).

Countertransference phenomena are often the result of the way in which the therapist interacts with the child in treatment. For example, the child may be seen as a victim, resulting in overemphasis on clarification of the parents' attitudes and motives rather than of the child's own feelings and motives. Often enough, the child is viewed as "innocent", revealing a judgemental attitude on the part of the therapist towards the child and his parents alike. As a consequence of this, the child's own contribution to the interaction is quite often neglected or not understood.

Countertransference can be connected with over-identification with the child, and with a denial of one's own aggression as well as that of the child (Piene et al., 1983). Such countertransference can interfere with the integration of the split-off parts of the child's internal objects as the therapist allies herself with the child's splitting, playing the "good mother" in therapy and leaving the "bad mother" split off outside therapy (Piene et al., 1983). On the other hand, therapists may sometimes rationalize some of their activities out of a wish to present themselves as models for identification, especially when they have to exercise the "auxiliary ego" function, as may be necessary with very young patients.

Rather than being a temporary activity, this is aimed at gratifying the patient's libidinal needs and the therapist's "good parent" countertransference. It is too easy to divert or manipulate the child's attention in order to relieve whatever uncomfortable affects the psychotherapist may have. Similarly, the therapist who is under stress in her current life and feels unprepared to respond to the child's emotional needs is more vulnerable towards the child's projections and may develop countertransference reactions towards the child as a depriving figure, identifying with the child's parents.

Among the parents of child patients, there will be some who induce feelings of competitiveness or even envy in the therapist. These are the parents who threaten the therapist's narcissism. They may be very wealthy individuals, people who are highly successful in their own professions, or they may even be colleagues bringing their children for treatment. Countertransference difficulties are more likely to occur when the patient is at the same stage as the therapist's children, or when the child reveals problems similar to those of the therapist's children or the therapist herself in childhood. In this case, the task of therapy may become contaminated by a wish for the child to love, respect, or admire the therapist more than the parent (Gabel & Bemporad, 1994).

In other cases, the child psychotherapist may be underestimated by angry parents or by cynical or aggressive parents. Here, because of countertransference, the therapist may be led to reject the family and classify it as untreatable in order to feel a sense of relief and reestablish her own self-esteem (Garber, 1992).

The sources of countertransference resistance in work with children and adolescents include: the need to be liked or to gratify the child, the need to be preoccupied with change and not experience sexual or aggressive feelings, the need for protection from the anxieties that are due to countertransference, and the wish to feel like a good parent.

We also know that the therapist may deny the existence of countertransference because of the threat to her narcissism. This is especially likely when her self-esteem is based on identification with an idealized parental figure, of whom the most recent is the therapist's own analyst. Countertransference feelings can be stirred up by the powerful regressive forces that become active in the child psychotherapist, who should be able to sample identifications without ceasing to function in accordance with her observing, working ego (Marcus, 1980).

Some therapists can adjust to certain kinds of behaviour and psychic structure in their patients, while others cannot. Child patients who are particularly aggressive or unresponsive in therapy easily arouse a sense of impotence in the therapist, who feels that her efforts and professional competence are being challenged. Instead of facing up to the limitations of the patient and her own frustration, the therapist may deny the difficulty by placing all the blame on the parents for creating such an unmanageable child. In this way, the therapist excuses the child, maintains her own self-image as an objective, caring, and competent clinician, and avoids having to face up to her countertransference (Gabel & Bemporad, 1994).

On other occasions—once more due to countertransference—the therapist may avoid setting limits when acting-out behaviour occurs and may even justify or misinterpret a sexual acting-out because of her unconscious need to perpetuate it. Out of envy and a competitive attitude towards the child, the therapist may sometimes stick rigidly to the rules or enforce a moralistic and excessively suppressive attitude, thus inhibiting the adolescent's emotional growth. Even diagnostic interviews can and do acquire positive and negative connotations under the influence of the therapist's emotional charge as a result of countertransference feelings. If, for example, the therapist is unable to deal with her countertransference reactions involving the arousal of violent feelings triggered by the overtly hostile reactions of the child, the diagnostic work is in danger and may be discontinued; at best, the child may be referred elsewhere. The same, of course, applies when similar countertransference reactions develop during therapy.

There is no doubt that the therapist should be aware of her vulnerability to countertransference and should be able to distinguish between countertransference proper and transference on the part of the therapist (Kohrman et al., 1971). The child psychotherapist should verify that her countertransference feelings towards the patient and the parents are appropriate and diagnostically useful, and that they are not her own personal transference towards the child and the parents (Wallace & Wallace, 1985). If this occurs, the therapist's empathy may well develop into over-identification with the child and/or the parents, blurring the distinction between the patient and the therapist's evoked childhood sense of self and thus blurring what are countertransference phenomena and what are reactions belonging solely to therapist's neurotic conflicts. If the therapist is not resisting, the content of countertransference may follow the course of empathic identifications with the patient and, consequently, of reactions to the patient's feelings, behaviour, and projections (McCarthy, 1989).

As far as psychotherapy with adolescents is concerned, Berman (1949) warned therapists to beware of "psychological blind spots" with respect to their own adolescent difficulties. Giovacchini, too, points out that severely disturbed young patients, who had traumatic infantile backgrounds with abandonment, rejection, and assault, perceive the therapist as non-empathic and depriving, thus causing great strain in the therapy (Giovacchini, 1985). Another interesting topic is that of the guilt felt by the therapist because she receives a fee when the adolescent patient does not talk during sessions and acts out his feelings outside the consulting-room without the therapist being able to understand and make the proper interpretations. This seems to be something that the therapist should clarify and understand by herself or with outside help.

It can be said, in general, that therapists find the sight of the child's sickness or neglect very hard to bear. It is very painful to tolerate the realization of the child's or adolescent's unhappiness, misery, and suffering, and this toleration can only be achieved if the therapist has worked through her own depression: otherwise, the situation may arise of the child psychotherapist being unable to permit the expression of strong psychic pain. It is interesting to speculate that the stress of the regressive pull on the therapist as she has to cope with the continual sexual and aggressive provocation of the children may be the reason why many therapists as they grow older tend to work less with children and adolescents (Schowalter, 1985). It also seems that when the therapist's reactions are not in tune with the patient's—in other words, if the unconsciously evoked countertransference feelings are not at a similar developmental stage, as in the case of the sexual countertransference developed by the therapist in response to transference feelings related to oral fixations—the countertransference stems from the therapist's unresolved conflicts.

The intensity of the transference may cause the therapist to feel as the child's parents have felt towards the patient, or to respond as the patient may have wished to be treated by his parents. The therapist's complementary position reflects the milieu in which the patient has lived, and which he recreates by regression. If instead of experiencing countertransference feelings the therapist acts out a part of the child's original experience, then the trauma is repeated. Such intense counter-transference reactions are reported in child therapy literature in the treatment of borderline and psychotic children (Palombo, 1985).

Finally, Schowalter (1985) discusses the countertransference phenomena and various other feelings that manifest themselves during therapy and stem from interaction between the therapist, the patient, and the patient's parents. He suggests that feelings of affection, admiration, idealization, or even latent seduction are generally less disruptive and less anxiety-provoking and so are less likely to come to attention. Similarly, competitive feelings towards parents or adolescents often go unnoticed. The counter-transference manifestations most likely to be noticed are those involving anger, hate, or fear, since these feelings are the most likely to cause either anxiety in the therapist or the abrupt discontinuation of therapy.

Close to the end of therapy, the regressive intensification of the transference, symptom revival, and mourning for the thera-pist as a transference object who has to be left may prove a hard test for the therapist's countertransference feelings. Therapists are usually more comfortable when making the decision to terminate therapy with young children, and less so with older children and adolescents, where they will tend to question the degree to which structural changes have been achieved. The therapist should become aware of her own separation anxiety and should not alter her therapeutic stance (Marcus, 1980).

Feelings of countertransference can thus be produced in the child and adolescent psychotherapist by the stimulation of feel-ings stemming from the therapist's own child self, from relations with the parents in her own family, and from the experiences of her own childhood. The entire therapeutic setting for the psycho- therapy of children and adolescents, including the psychopa- thology of the child and the participation and attitude of the parents, militates in favour of this. We also have to bear in mind the environmental factors in the therapist's life as well as the motives that may have led her to make the choice of her profes- sion. All the above factors may affect the therapist's vulnerability to countertransference reactions. The feelings of countertrans- ference can have a positive or negative impact on every stage of the therapy, from diagnosis all the way through the therapeutic procedure until its termination.

Conclusions

This brief and selected review of the literature demonstrates that there was a long delay in understanding the useful significance of countertransference in the psychotherapy of children and adolescents. Today, however, it occupies a central position in dealing with the therapeutic problems that appear in the work with children and adolescents and also in the therapist's under- standing and effectiveness of intervention.

Countertransference seems to be a natural and inevitable part of therapy. In the case of the psychotherapy of children and adolescents, it is widely recognized as a very useful tool in understanding the patient—not just as a facilitating instrument, but as an essential component in the progress of the therapeutic process.

The following main types of countertransference phenomena can be discerned, in terms of their source:

1. a variety of countertransference feelings evoked by the child or adolescent, according to his stage of development and specific psychopathology;

2. countertransference feelings evoked by the parents in rela- tion to the child and the therapist;

3. countertransference feelings evoked by the therapist herself, which may originate in the therapist's internalized parents,

the child part of the therapist, or unresolved conflict and fantasies in search of gratification.

The personality and the overall internal world of the therapist are undoubtedly always involved in countertransference, as are re-actions triggered by the particular nature of the circumstances and by the patients and their setting which would probably cause countertransference feelings in any psychotherapist.

Psychoanalytic psychotherapy could be described as a meet-ing between the psyches of two individuals in a setting that permits the patient to travel along a fantasy route escorted—discreetly and helpfully—by the therapist. As has often been said, the therapist's instruments are her self, her sensibility, and her intuition, which allow her to share the psychic world of the patient. It follows that there will always be feelings that this process evokes in the therapist alone, and that there will always be a need for deeper understanding of the mechanisms by which the feelings of transference and countertransference are generated and interact. The study of the human soul is an endless undertaking—which is probably true, also, of the study of countertransference.

CHAPTER TWO

Thoughts on countertransference and observation

Judith Trowell

Countertransference has become one of the most important and most useful tools in psychoanalytic work. In order to work effectively with children, young people, adults, groups, or organizations, one needs to know, understand, and be able to use one's countertransference. Others still question the whole concept, either on the basis that it has *no* meaning or no clarity of meaning, or that it is used so extensively and is applied so widely that everything can be taken as part of the countertransference. It is likely that this questioning and distancing from the ideas of countertransference would mean that, in the clinical setting, important material or issues are not given the significance and importance they merit if one is trying to treat the whole person.

Freud struggled with the idea of countertransference. He felt that the feelings aroused in the analyst by the patient were due to the analyst's own unanalysed emotional issues and that these needed to be acknowledged by the analyst and worked through but kept separate from the work with the patient. This is in contrast to the transference, where feelings of the patient related to earlier or external relationships are transferred on to the therapist. Initially Freud also saw this as an impediment, a hindrance to the analytic work, but later he came to see this same transference phenomena as a useful therapeutic tool. Countertransference, he remained clear, was to do with the analyst's own issues. This view prevailed for some time, and some very eminent analysts—for example D. W. Winnicott and Melanie Klein—remained of the view that countertransference relates to the analyst's own issues, although both of them made major contributions to our understanding of the psychic processes and mechanisms occurring between patient and therapist.

Paula Heimann (1950) wrote her major paper "On Counter-transference" distinguishing between those feelings that arise in the analyst because of their own issues and those feelings that arise in the analyst that are a communication from the patient about their own affective state. This communication is generally at an unconscious level and is thought to be mediated by projection and projective identification or by different types of projective identification—for example, evocative or acquisitive (Britton, 1989; Spillius, 1992). Pearl King (1978) had explored this in her consideration of the affective response of the analyst, and since then there has been a vast amount of thinking and writing about the countertransference, with the particularly helpful conceptualizations of Bion, Rosenfeld, and Sandler.

Working with children, often young children of 5 years and under, highlights the importance of countertransference. It is also in this area that it seems to me that most of the learning of trainees about countertransference occurs, because of the development of observation training.

Observation

Arising out of all the observational studies of infants and young children that were taking place in Vienna at the time of Freud (Steiner, 1994), Esther Bick (1964) developed infant and young-child observation as a training experience for those wishing to work psychoanalytically with children and young people. This observation training has grown and developed and is a part of most psychoanalytically based child therapy trainings and is now being used as a training tool in many other disciplines and professions (Brafman, 1988; Miller, Rustin, & Shuttleworth, 1989; Trowell & Miles, 1991; Trowell & Rustin, 1991).

Observation (that is, observing an infant or young child with its carers) can teach the observer a great deal, about child development, family interaction, and different care-giving styles in racial and cultural settings, but above all trainees learn about countertransference. Observing for an hour a week, then writing up their process recording and then presenting their observation in a small seminar group is a very intense and very powerful experience. The issues, particularly countertransference, become starkly obvious, and because the observation and seminar occur weekly for at least an academic year, sufficient safety and trust can be established to allow exploration of the countertransference.

When trainees present their observation material, they are talking about situations in which they are not expected to intervene or interpret but are expected to respond as a concerned human being, a participant observer. These parameters seem to provide a setting in which the countertransference as a phenomenon can be discovered whilst the situation is such that the subject and the trainee are protected from any enactment—or at least any serious or damaging acting out or acting in.

Peter

The observer is visiting a family consisting of a mother, a father who is rarely seen, and two children—Peter, a boy of 3½ who is the subject of the observation; David, a second boy, who is now 10 months old. There is a dog and a cat in the family. This vignette is well into the observation, which began when David was a few weeks old.

Meanwhile . . . we enter the sitting-room, via the kitchen, as Peter is behind the door that leads in from the hall; David is all smiles, he had made a protesting noise when Mother placed him on the hall floor. Now he greets me with a beaming smile. Mother comments on this, observing that he's been complaining for the past hour. We sit on armchairs, Mother has David on his feet, supported by her arms. He makes growling noises. The dog greets me with warmth and wagging tail. The dog deposits a ball at my feet, I roll it with my foot, the dog retrieves it immediately. I whisper a greeting to the dog, as Peter is stretched on a floor cushion watching television. David "speaks" in a whisper too. He makes noises through his lips (like a mild raspberry), the dog now pushing his nose against my hand to get me to stroke him.

David leans against his mother's knee, laughing in my direction and making (joyful) crowing noises, then buries his head in mother's lap. Peter's television programme has ended, he wanders past us on the chairs. On his way back, he stands on the hearth and asks his mother to move her slippered foot "over here, please". She says no, and says it is too far to stretch. Peter says "just try . . . then I want to step on it". Mum, laughing, refuses to move her foot, and then immediately does, and Peter presses on her toes. The dog has moved very near to me, with the ball, begging to be played with. She is a very comic dog. I'm trying to ignore her, but it is hard. Mother sends her to lie down. Peter has now climbed on to Mum's lap, and lies on his tummy. David is sublimely unworried by his bigger brother climbing over him to lie on Mum. Mother says, "there's a bottom to smack", and Peter screams with delight, and mock fear. He climbs behind her on the arm chair. Mother involves David, "Where's he gone?", places her hand behind her and tickles Peter tummy; Peter laughs loudly, wriggling to escape. "Can't think where he's got to." David peeks around Mum to see Peter. The dog presents the ball to me once more, having crept away from her basket. I give it a gentle roll, and she follows it. Peter is now endeavouring to use his feet to push Mum off the chair. He tries quite hard. She resists, and he once more flexes his muscles to push her. She protests. David has now discovered the knitted pattern on Mum's jumper, and has started to touch the buttonholes, etc.

Mum continues to tickle Peter so he is too weak to push her off the chair. Peter begs her to stop, "I can't cope with it". Mum then sighs and says to no-one in particular that she doesn't know how she manages, with so many needing attention (this includes the dog and cat) and threatens to sell Peter at the Market. She begins to hold David upside down; Peter climbs around and says "Give him to me". Mum refuses and says, "I don't want him to be squashed". He says once more, "Give him to me". She swivels in her chair and puts David on Peter's lap in the armchair. David begins to protest once more, as he leaves his mother's hold. "Have you got him?" Peter, very self-possessed, assures her that he has. Peter tries to play "on your back" with David, but he cries. Mum lifts him up. Peter moves onto the centre of the floor and starts to wrestle with a cushion. Somehow, he is crying quite painfully; Mum doesn't notice immediately, being engaged with leaning over David on the floor, but once she notices that Peter is really distressed, she asks what he's done to hurt himself. He says it's his leg but is unclear, through the sobs, as to how it occurred. Mum rubs his leg, then speculates whether she has the wrong one. She queries Peter, "Is this the one? Is this the one?" Peter says "no" both times; she then rubs his elbow and asks if it is his arm. She tickles him a little and he laughs. David begins to complain, he only makes noises, but they effectively convey his protests. She turns her attention to David. Peter picks up the cushion, very angrily, and throws it down, as if to punish it; he lifts it once more, and slams it down with force, towards Mum. She's aware of it but is occupied with David. Peter hits her with it again. "Stop it", and "have you finished?". The question is quiet but serious. Peter stretches towards the cushion; it is within reach if he leans more, but he says, "Gone too far away . . ." Peter then turns his attention to the baby walker, and lays over it.

Mother mentions something about anything for a quiet life. Peter shouts out loudly at that (he's moved round towards the toy-box behind me), evidently taking her words literally. He makes another loud whoop. Mum quietens him, and then suggests he goes upstairs to find a book so she can read him a story. In fact she suggests two books, one to read, and one to see the pictures. He goes out, having asked "in a minute?", and she reiterating that he'll hear the story later. Peter says "Now". Mother "No", and then she says, "that will keep him busy".

David looks at me sideways, eating the plastic dog on wheels, laughing. Now he's blowing bubbles. Peter returns with one book. "All we have time for", he says. He goes over to Mum, who has moved over to the sofa. He asks her to read it. She says, "No, I'm busy". As she patently isn't, she then sings "Busy doing nothing, nothing the whole day through. . . ." David is now rattling a plastic box.

The remainder of the observation was spent watching a television programme and Mother was on the telephone. Mother then read a story to both children.

The discussion in the seminar group was lively, the group and the observer finding it both a pleasant, ordinary family session but also aware of an unease that had been growing over a number of observations. The observer suddenly became quite acutely distressed. In previous seminars we had been aware of the issues for this observer: she, herself a working mother, was upset about her need to leave her own children and miss out on their development, and so observing someone else spending time with their children was painful. She was also aware that she as an older child herself very much identified with the older son and his feelings of being pushed out by the new baby. But today there was something else. Gradually we explored that perhaps the observer was in touch with something that was preoccupying mother. The observation did not appear to differ dramatically from previous ones, but what was different was the observer's response. Two weeks later, Mother cancelled the observation session because she was going into hospital to have a termination. The observer was shaken but also relieved because now it all made sense, and her own self-questioning and uncertainty could be thought about. Looking back over the observations, the seminar group could see clues in the material, but what was most powerful was the intense emotional reaction of the observer.

This quite small experience of countertransference does seem to be part of the gradual evolution of an understanding of and then some confidence in the capacity to be in touch through the countertransference.

Clinical Work

The countertransference is so important and so useful because of its use clinically. I will give two examples.

Darren

The first example is *an assessment* with a boy, Darren, who had been physically abused six years before. He had been beaten, bones had been broken, and he had been locked in the cupboard under the stairs for hours. At 12 years he was very small and pre-pubertal, and he was so defiant, disruptive, and difficult that he had been excluded from school and his foster placement was breaking down.

> Darren came with me very eagerly and seemed very eager to talk. He talked and talked about his own, real, parents. He had gone on and on, hoping they would get back together again and he could go back to them (he had been received into care and shortly afterwards his parents had split up). He explained that every time he looked at his foster parents he got angry because they were not his real parents. He told me he lay awake most nights until at least midnight thinking about his natural parents and the future. What was he to do? He was supposed to see his real father every three months, but often father didn't turn up. He said he was angry about what had happened and angry that father had another girl-friend, but he knew his father loved him. His father stole to try and get enough money to have Darren live with him. Darren was vehement that girls grow up like their mothers and boys like their fathers, so he was just messing about in and out of trouble; what was the point, his father was in prison again now.

> He said he had seen his real mother again after a very long gap; she didn't want him to know where she was. He was very upset when she said he couldn't come and live with them. He was determined to find her when he was 18, but what if she has died by then? He said that if he knew where she was, he would run off there.

He said he resented his foster-parents very much, but he became upset as he told me they has decided not to adopt him. He was convinced that soon he would have no parents. He thought that a lot of the time there was no point in anything, he wasn't wanted by anyone. When he felt like that he got angry and messed everything up, was rude to the teachers, hit the other children, destroyed things. He wondered if it would be better if he didn't exist.

I asked if he talked about all this to anyone, and he said no, he just thought things in his head, daydreams, he was just angry or upset all the time. He ended by saying he knew his foster-parents had done everything they could, he just couldn't accept what they offered. They weren't his real parents.

This boy showed how, beneath his self-assured, defiant exterior, he was very sad and aware, and possibly suicidal. When I saw him a second time, he did not acknowledge these feelings and spent the time being rude and contemptuous and trying to demolish my room and possessions, toys, etc. He did agree that both the gap between the two assessment sessions, and his realization that I could only see him a few times, left him feeling I was the same as other adults, with little to give. This left him thinking, "What's the point, it's all hopeless and useless."

Reflecting after these assessment sessions was very painful, as was drawing together information from other sources—his social worker, foster parents, and school. In the first session I had felt his need and vulnerability, but also that he had some capacity for awareness, insight, and understanding and that he was a boy who could engage with me. In the second session I had felt pushed away, dismissed as rubbish, useless. I realized I had expected the second session to be a time when we built on the first, to understand and think about his predicament further, so that I could think with him about what might be helpful. All my expectation had felt shattered by his contempt and destructiveness, and I was left feeling rejected and then angry and relieved that I did not have to see him again.

But, as I reflected more, I began to be aware of an overwhelming sadness and heaviness; I realized that part of me wanted to say, it's all right, I'll look after him, take him on for intensive therapy. I was very aware then that I was in touch with the desperate, needy, raging boy, or small child that was terrified of being abandoned. Alongside this, however, I was also aware of a quite cruel cutting, sadistic feeling that was outraged and determined to destroy in a triumphant way.

It seemed to me that these countertransference feelings were very important in talking with the foster-parents and in planning his future treatment needs. As well as the vulnerable, quite thoughtful boy, and the angry defiant boy, there was the raging, desperate small child and the triumphant sadistic aspect. Intensive therapy for Darren and work with the foster-mother did lead to improvement. The foster-parents felt that our acknowledging his triumphant sadism made it more possible for them to make sense of how they felt and to persist with him rather than send him away.

Lucy

My second example is a treatment case. Lucy was seen because of great concern in the nursery class, and her mother was also concerned. Lucy, aged 3½ years, lived alone with her mother. There had been concerns about Lucy's father, who had disappeared; the mother was flat and depressed, and she was seen once weekly in parallel with Lucy's treatment. Lucy was seen three times weekly.

Mother finds Lucy very difficult, she feels that you can't get through to her. Lucy is cut off, somewhere else, although she is there physically. Lucy is rather remote and detached, not showing any affection. There were initial difficulties with separation. The session that I describe now was after separation had been established.

On her own, Lucy didn't play with the animals, doll, or plasticine, and didn't draw. She spent the whole time with a jigsaw. This meant Lucy pointed to a piece and I had to suggest the next piece to it. She had reasonable manual dexterity and coordination in putting them together but could not "see" the next piece herself.

As she did the jigsaw she began to talk, about her school and what she did there, her home, and her Mummy. After a while

I made a comment about Daddy, she had been saying Mummy was always busy and cried a lot. Immediately, she was different. She talked and talked about Daddy. Lucy sees her father often. Daddy is there every day. She talks to him and told me about all the things he did, but it all felt strange and bizarre to me. I decided to ask whether she had any frightening or worrying things. She didn't respond until I asked about bed and night-time, and whether she had bad dreams. The whole of the rest of the time was filled by Lucy talking and talking about monsters that come to her bedroom and hit her, not in the night when she is asleep but when she is awake. The monsters come in or they are hiding under her bed.

She continued that Daddy is there, he protects her, he frightens them away, but they keep coming back. Daddy comes every evening and in the daytime too because the monsters come into the garden and the house. They don't come to school. The monsters didn't come into my room (I asked). She went on and on about the monsters hitting her, beating her up, and Daddy protecting her. It was not clear whether she sees or hears the monsters, but she certainly "sees", "hears", and talks to Daddy.

During this account she was looking at me and was very much in contact with me, though animated and frightened. However, as the session came to an end, Lucy had gone—she became flat, lifeless, and withdrawn. It had ended sooner than I realized (the time had flown by). I said perhaps she needed me to help her, to make it safe. I said maybe she might worry the monsters would be angry she had talked about them and perhaps she felt frightened. She dismissed me—Daddy would protect her.

After this session I found myself quite unable to think. I felt as though I must be crazy, I did not know how to make sense of this session when father was clearly present, and yet my understanding was that father had disappeared. It seemed to me that her father was providing the supportive parenting and that mother was either absent or needing to be looked after. Gradually my capacity to think returned; I restrained myself from telephoning social services to enquire if father was back in the home. I did talk to my co-worker, and we tried to make sense of the material. Lucy needed to engage me, keep me alert and involved, presumably as she did with her mother—hence the jigsaw behaviour. Once I was paying attention, the fear and terror could be conveyed to me as well as her desperate need for a Daddy person to keep her safe—her wish that I would become this and her anger and distress that I did not.

But my intense anxiety, and the feeling that I needed to act to protect her and the awareness that I felt I was going mad, seemed to me to be my response to her communication at an unconscious level that there were unthinkable, overwhelming experiences for her that she could not deal with or process.

My co-worker talked of her awareness of the mother's depression and fragile hold on reality at times, she had wondered if the mother might be suicidal. She was also struggling with the mother's rage and envy because Lucy was having help. That mother's own childhood had been very difficult and no-one had noticed her suffering.

A part of a session some time later: Lucy started—"Let's make a boat—you remember how it was." Then she told me how to do it and began to make it. I said "it was nearly holiday time and the boat was perhaps a floating home that would keep us together during the holiday because it might be painful to think about her going away and that I would be away. The boat could be a way of keeping us together in her mind."

"What do you mean?" I said, "Well, you will be away from the Clinic and I will also be away, and if you miss coming, we know from before that you get angry and upset, so I thought the boat might be your way of making it easier." "I'm going to Devon." I said, "Yes, that sound's good, but I'm wondering if you are wondering about me." "Well, you are with yourself." I said, "You would like me to be here waiting to see you, but you know that the Clinic Dr Trowell has a home and there may be a daddy there and boys and girls."

"Shut up—I need the loo." She went off and did a wee.

On her return she reeled off a list of Mr Men books, enquiring in detail if I knew them. Some I did, some I didn't. I said I was wondering if she was trying to find out by asking about the books if I had contact with other boys and girls, and this had followed talking about daddies and other children. She spun round and she stood up. "I can fly". She flapped her arms. I said it seemed as though she wished she could fly and she was trying but it was pretending, and in fact she couldn't. She took some paper and she said she was drawing lots of poohs coming out of a bottom. I wondered if she had thoughts like that, flying, when she played with her bottom. She was very flushed. "How did you know I played with my bottom?" I said, well boys and girls do play with their bottoms, but she had also had a daddy who had perhaps done things to her bottom, and I wondered if, when her bottom was touched, she found herself thinking she could do magic—fly. After a pause, I added maybe she was wondering about me, did I want excitement or could I bear the rubbish feelings, the no-good feelings.

In this I think Lucy is showing that she has begun to be able to think. This seemed to develop as I became more able to bear the awfulness and confusion. The pain was becoming less frantic, much sadder, but again I needed to be very in touch to clarify my own and her issues.

Discussion

The most important consideration when thinking about the countertransference in working with children and adolescents is how well one can observe oneself. As analysts and therapists, our patients provoke feelings to do with our own childhoods and our own parenting of our own children. In these clinical examples, the most important skill I drew on to aid my clinical work was my capacity to observe the child and to observe myself. With both Darren and Lucy I could all too easily have acted out, done something. This intense projective identification can be very difficult to resist—it easily hooks onto one's own rescue fantasies. Thinking about what is going on, the hopelessness, the pain, the rage, the manic flight, can appear straightforward.

Struggling with the many borderline and very disturbed and traumatized children and young people means that the therapist must be able to understand very early mechanisms, the use of fantasy, splitting, denial, projection, and projective identification. These were in operation with Darren and Lucy. Observation skills seem essential if these processes are to be grappled with in analytic work. They enable the analyst or therapist to integrate information coming from the patient, both conscious and unconscious, and information from within. Internal work can then enable the analyst or therapist to unravel the transference and countertransference in the room and then reflect upon an appropriate interpretation.

CHAPTER THREE

Reflections on transference, countertransference, session frequency, and the psychoanalytic process

Alex Holder

The somewhat clumsy title of my chapter serves the purpose of drawing attention to a number of factors and phenomena in our clinical practice which are correlated in specific ways, and which I would like to explore here. It is my contention that the number of sessions we work analytically with a child or adolescent during a week has a crucial bearing on the development or emergence of transference phenomena and on the corresponding intensity and depth of countertransference responses, and thus frequency influences and determines the kind of analytic process that evolves in the course of time.

If at all possible, I would like to avoid any value judgements of the kind that four or five sessions a week are better than one or two, although I realize that it is difficult to avoid such implications altogether. My aim is, rather, to explore the *differences* that arise in different settings—differences in the quality of the relationship between child and therapist which develop, differences in the momentum that the psychoanalytic process gains and the depths that it reaches, and differences in the realm of the transference–countertransference dynamics and, with it, the therapist's ability to get in touch with her patient's unconscious to promote the process of understanding and interpretation.

For the sake of information, I would like to interpolate at this point that during the first twenty years of my analytic work with children and adolescents at the Anna Freud Centre in London, I mostly worked in high-frequency settings—that is, with five sessions a week. For the last ten years or so I have worked in Hamburg, with a radical change to mostly twice-weekly therapies. This is the usual setting adopted by those who train as child and adolescent psychotherapists in Germany, and it is influenced by the terms of the health insurances. However, I do not want to enlarge on this issue here, since it is not directly relevant to my topic, except to say that these conditions discourage therapists from attempting to carry out high-frequency treatments with children and adolescents. It is a different matter when it comes to the analytic treatment of adults, although even here the health insurances now pay for only three sessions a week, arguing that there is no scientific evidence as yet that a fourth session makes a treatment more effective.

We all know how difficult—if not impossible—it is in our impossible profession to prove anything. We can only convey impressions, perhaps convictions, that we have gained from our various clinical experiences; and since I have had considerable experience of both high-frequency and low-frequency treatments with children and adolescents, this is precisely what I hope to be able to do in this presentation.

I would like to begin with some general remarks and considerations about transference and countertransference. It goes without saying that they are ubiquitous phenomena in our daily lives. In this sense, we all respond to the transferences of others onto us, with countertransference reactions. As analysts, we may contemplate on what is happening between us and others in daily life; that is, we may try to gain a deeper understanding of certain interpersonal dynamics. But the ordinary citizen is not usually interested in such understanding—he or she just acts and reacts in particular ways.

We owe it to Freud's genius to have made these phenomena— in particular that of the transference—into cornerstones of psychoanalytic technique and understanding. For adults, he introduced a special setting—the couch on which the patient lies and behind which the analyst sits, out of sight—a setting that is meant to facilitate regressive fantasies and the emergence and development of transference phenomena in the patient, and to give the therapist sufficient space and peace for her own reflections on what is going on.

With children, such a setting is not possible. We are always face to face with our children, whether we do analysis or therapy, and we are always more or less active in our work with children, whether we take on roles assigned to us, help the child in some play activity, play games with him, and so on. One of the questions that arises at this point is: what are the repercussions of this difference in setting on the development of the transference? Are we as much, or as exclusively, transference objects for the child as we are for an adult, or do we always remain—to a lesser or greater extent—a real, new object for a child? Melanie Klein and her followers always maintained that everything that occurs between patient and analyst has a transference meaning. Others—and I count myself amongst them—have not shared this view and have emphasized instead that, in addition to being a transference object for the child, we also perform a significant function as a new object with whom the child has new experiences and can thus make important new identifications.

I would like to draw attention to another important difference regarding transferences in work with children as opposed to adults. With the latter, the most important objects that feed the transference dynamics during treatment belong to the past and exist in the patient only as internal objects. With children, this is usually very different. They continue to live with and to be dependent on their primary objects—their parents, siblings, grandparents, and so forth—relationships that in themselves have a longer or shorter history and of which facets will appear in the transferences onto the therapist, although it is not always easy to be certain whether we are dealing with the revival of a past object relationship in the here-and-now of the analytic setting or with a straightforward transfer of a current dynamic with one of the primary objects. Furthermore, some of the emotional cathexis always remains with these objects and is not totally transferred onto the therapist.

On the basis of my own experience, I would say that, generally speaking, this differentiation between past and present transferences becomes easier with a higher frequency of sessions. I see the reasons for this as an important difference between high- and low-frequency treatments—namely, one that concerns the readiness for regression. I choose the word "readiness" deliberately in order to suggest that all children have the *capacity* to regress but often resist such regressions when the conditions are not favourable. And this, in my view, is the case when the sessions are spaced out too much, as is the case, for instance, with a twice-weekly setting when three or four days lie between sessions. On the other hand, if sessions are almost daily, and once a child has settled down into treatment, he usually feels secure enough to reveal more regressive features of the internal object relationships during sessions. To put it differently: with a high frequency of sessions, a child is more likely to feel secure that its anxieties and other affects associated with regressive functioning can be contained by the analyst and the setting.

Jenny

In order to illustrate this, I would like to bring a short clinical vignette. It comes from the analysis of a girl whom I shall call Jenny. She started analysis when she was just 6 years old. She suffered from what looked like a school phobia, but it turned out to be a need to return home to ascertain that she had not omnipotently killed her mother. She was also provocative, at other times depressive, and there were indications of a severe superego. Treatment showed that she had enormous difficulties in accepting that she was a girl. It made her feel worthless, and her self-esteem suffered accordingly. After about half a year of treatment, the transference relationship got more and more coloured by anal qualities, reflected in a need to attack, control, and devalue me and attempts at symbolically castrating me by cutting off my tie and my hair or breaking my glasses. This development reached a climax when she was 7, and she decided to write a story on "How Mr Holder was a poo". She stapled some pieces of paper together into a booklet and wrote the following story, illustrating it with appropriate pictures as she went along:

"Mr Holder smells up his bottom. Here is Mr Holder's bottom and his penice [sic] with his wee wee coming out. This is Mr Holder's poo poo. Look at Mr Holder's red poo poo. Look at Mr

Holder's big fat green face and mauve eyes. Look at Mr Holder's brown wee wee. Look at Mr Holder's silly black hair. Mr Holder's raincoat smells so much. Just look at it. Look at Mr Holder's silly umbrella. Mr Holder's poo is coming out of his penice [sic]. Look at Mr Holder's wee wee coming out of his bottom. Look at Mr Holder's blue blood. All Mr Holder's things smell. So that was why Mr Holder was a poo."

It is my contention that the writing of such a story, with its primary process elements and regressive confusions, would not have been possible without the preceding sustained transference development in that direction over several weeks, in which the projection of Jenny's devalued self-image onto me and her consequent denigration of me played a significant part.

On the other hand, this story also marked a turning-point in Jenny's analysis in that it was the beginning of a greater readiness on her part towards verbalization and writing rather than action, accompanied by a gradual move to a phallic–oedipal level when she made us joint authors in the writing of plays and stories, and we thus produced symbolic babies together.

If we accept that what a child does or says during a session is a surface manifestation of some aspect of its inner world, however defensively distorted by the time it reaches conscious expression, then it follows that it is our chief task to understand the unconscious or latent meaning of these communications and to share this understanding with the child at an appropriate time and in an appropriate form. In this respect, it is similar to proceeding from the manifest to the latent content of a dream. At the same time we have to tune in to the possible transference implications of what the child does or says. This is by no means an easy task when we bear in mind the defensive modifications and distortions that any mental content may have undergone by the time it reaches conscious expression: the object may be changed, the affect reversed, the drive content regressively distorted, an aspect of the self may be projectively located in someone else, guilt feelings may be evaded by blaming others—there is an infinite number of possible constellations to be considered and monitored by the therapist in which she is guided by her countertransference reactions.

If we are honest with ourselves, are we not sometimes at a loss, at the end of a session, to know exactly what it was really all about, at least at the deepest level of its unconscious significance? Johan Norman has pointed out—and I share his view—that it is not only the child who needs time to reveal his unconscious wishes and fantasies but that we, as therapists, also need time to get in tune and in touch, via our empathy and countertransference, with that child's unconscious inner world. I would like to quote a brief passage from his comments on "Frequency in Child and Adolescent Analysis" which he made at the Standing Conference of the European Psychoanalytical Federation on Child and Adolescent Analysis:

> The analyst has to become involved in the fantasies of the patient, has to play the patient's game, to learn how the game is going, in order to understand how to step out of the game, a step the patient is unable to take without the analyst's help. The analyst, because he is involved, can find the way out. The analyst needs the intensity of the relation in which the patient's unconscious is allowed to have an effect on the analyst's unconscious so as to create the involvement which the analyst can understand and find his way out of.
>
> The patient needs the greater frequency to develop the hope, the illusion, that he can win the analyst over to his case; the analyst must be so important for the patient that he becomes the only and last hope. The analyst needs the greater frequency so as to be caught up in the unconscious fantasies of the patient and through his involvement find a way out of the involvement and the unconscious game of the patient. [Norman, 1993, p. 60]

The amount of time and space evoked in this quotation is, however, not at our disposal when we see a child infrequently, bearing in mind that low-frequency therapies do not, as a rule, last longer than those with a high frequency—on the contrary. So the total time spent with the child in twice-weekly therapy tends to be considerably less than half the time spent together in a high-frequency setting. And I think that the overall length of a treatment also plays an important part in terms of the goals that can be achieved.

But it is not only a question of the time alone. What also plays a crucial role is the fact of continuity and density. In this respect,

I have noticed a considerable difference between my analytical experiences in London and my therapeutic ones in Hamburg. With the close daily proximity of sessions in the London analyses, the unfolding of a particular theme over a number of sessions was far more common than I found to be the case in the therapies that I have conducted since, with the result that the process of tuning into a child's unconscious and deepening my understanding of its messages has become more difficult and fragmented, if not to say more limited in the long run.

I would like to illustrate this problem with a clinical vignette from the psychotherapy of an 8-year-old girl who has been coming to treatment twice a week for about one and a half years now because of her problems of coping with the separation from her ambivalently loved father who, on account of his violent temper and physical punishment of the children, had been thrown out of the home by the mother about a year previously. In addition, she, Miranda, and her twin brother, Martin, had a very hostile relationship with each other. Martin has also been offered treatment, and his two sessions take place at the same time as his sister's, with a female colleague of mine whose room is opposite my consulting-room.

Miranda

In a recent session, Miranda, not for the first time, decided to play princess. As on previous occasions, she put two chairs on top of each other. This is her throne. I am assigned the role of her servant who has to help her climb up to the throne, who has to bring her "dry white wine" (her mother works as a secretary in a wine firm), who has to hand her nail-varnish etc., and who gets generally ordered about by her. On previous occasions, her defensive reversal of roles had been interpreted, as well as her underlying anger at feeling dominated by her strict mother. On this occasion, her dramatization took a new turn. After having had to play the role of servant for a while, I had to change my hat and become a messenger who announced the arrival of a prince. Then I had to impersonate the prince, who had come to invite her to a dinner and dance at his castle, an invitation that she gladly accepted. So I thought that we had moved into an oedipal situation, from a mother-transference to a father-transference. I interpreted her wish for me to make her into my wife. I did not, on this occasion, verbalize her wish to get rid of my actual wife, of whose existence Miranda knows and against whom she had expressed hostile and destructive sentiments on previous occasions.

At the end of the session, which took place on a Thursday, I felt that we were on our way to further work on her oedipal conflicts, including the idealization of her father in the transference of whom she was, in fact, frightened, partly because of her own experiences with him, partly because she had identified with her mother's somewhat paranoid fears that he might abduct the children to a Far East country where he originally came from, although he was now living in Hamburg and had, in the meantime, remarried and produced another daughter.

But when Miranda came back for her next session the following Monday, the princess theme was far away. She had arrived with a plastic bag, out of which she took some material which she had started to sew together into a bag, meant to be an Easter present for her mother. Although I did make some comments about the reparative significance of her present in view of the wishes she had expressed the previous week, Miranda reacted as though she did not know what I was talking about and clearly was not interested in pursuing the matter any further. She wanted to get on with her bag, occasionally enlisting my help when running into difficulties on her own. She was unusually quiet during the session, as though preoccupied with something she could not share with me.

It is perhaps idle to speculate what might have happened if this session had taken place on Friday, the day after the previous one. I could imagine that the oedipal material that had surfaced on Thursday might still have been more alive in Miranda's mind then—that is, still be emotionally invested—and might not yet have been subjected to so much defensive activity as seemed the case four days later. With such a gap in time, the momentum that had been reached in a previous session is often lost, and greater resistances have re-established themselves. For this reason, some therapists who work with two or three sessions a week prefer to place them on successive days in order to facilitate continuity through proximity, even though this means longer time gaps between the clusters of sessions. But whichever solution is adopted in distributing the two or three sessions during a week, one cannot avoid the fact that the more continuous flow of material and the greater persistence of specific themes or conflicts is interfered with, as is, for that matter, the continuity and flow of the work of interpretation on our side.

At this point, I would like to quote some pertinent comments by James Gammill, who has had a similar experience to mine except that he moved from London—where he received his child analytical training—first to the Unites States and then to France. In his introduction to a panel on the question of frequency in child and adolescent analysis at the Standing Conference mentioned above, he wrote, comparing his experiences in child analysis and therapy:

> However, . . . certain areas could not be as successfully reached and treated with psychotherapy as with psychoanalysis. For example, there is far less opportunity for the *elaboration of fantasies*, in which the same underlying fantasy can find multiple forms and combinations, analogous to myths with all their variations. The *deepening of the transference*, which is so important in the analysis of the neuroses, is more difficult and less complete in psychotherapy. . . . Notwithstanding that analytic psychotherapy may lead to much understanding and relief of symptoms and even to the expansion and enrichment of the personality, hidden areas, concealing aspects of the multiple origins of phobias, are less likely to be located and explored than in the analytic situation. [Gammill, 1992, p. 100]

Gammill looks at and describes the situation as it arises on the child's side, emphasizing in particular the limitations on the elaboration of fantasies in psychotherapy as well as those affecting the deepening of the transference. I would like to add that there are corresponding limitations on the side of the therapist which we might subsume under the heading of the "deepening of the countertransference", which would include the elaboration of fantasies about the child, its inner world, and its unconscious way of functioning. I addressed this very point in a previous paper on child analysis and analytical child psychotherapy:

> The more frequent and denser the regular contacts between child and therapist are, the more intense becomes the emotional significance of the mutual relationship. I would like to emphasize above all the mutuality of this phenomenon: It is not only the child who cathects his therapist highly in such a constellation and assigns him a relatively large space in its inner life, but the therapist himself is preoccupied with such a child much more intensely, and it occupies a much broader space in *his* inner life as well. One probably arrives at a wrong estimate in this respect if one limits oneself to the conscious realm. We should assume instead that very many processes which have to do with such a mutual relationship occur on a descriptively unconscious level. [Holder, 1991, p. 411]

I would *now* complement the aspect of the inner space occupied by the child in the therapist and, vice versa, by that of the "inner presence" which each has for the other. One of the implications of the foregoing considerations is that I have given the notion of countertransference a somewhat wider meaning, limiting it not only to the immediate inner responses of the therapist to the child's material during a session, but extending it to the elaborations that occur unconsciously between sessions and may affect the overall emotional attitude in which one meets a particular patient for the next session. Since much of this elaboration occurs outside of consciousness, it is all the more important to monitor and scrutinize one's inner emotional climate towards the patient before or at the beginning of a session.

With Miranda, for instance, there have been occasions when I became aware of a reluctance or unwillingness on my part to collect her from the waiting-room for her session. It became clear to me that this always happened when the previous session had been unsatisfactory for one reason or another in my own estimation—be it that she was rather resistant, that I felt that I did not understand what was going on, or that she had been rather provocative, had transgressed limits, and thus had aroused considerable anger in me. It was only on some of these occasions that I—during or after the previous session—was conscious of my negative countertransference to her not being an easy patient, but this only surfaced in my resistance to fetching her for the next session.

A very subtle variation of such a countertransference response may come into operation when we agree to carry out a treatment in a setting that is different from the one we initially considered to be optimal, or, even more so, if for one reason or another a chosen setting changes in the course of treatment. One therefore has to think very carefully before entering into some sort of compromise with parents or with an adolescent, such as agreeing to undertake the treatment with fewer sessions a week than one had considered necessary after the diagnostic investigations.

I would like to give a brief example of the second kind—that is, involving a change in the setting during the course of an ongoing treatment.

Andrew

Some years ago, I began the analysis of a 6-year-old adopted boy. After having been very much neglected by his biological mother during the first year of his life, Andrew was placed in a home for the next two years, then adopted by a childless couple. When he was 5, his adoptive parents separated, Andrew remaining with his adoptive mother. But there were regular and frequent contacts with his adoptive father. A colleague of mine who had done the diagnostic investigation recommended an analysis for Andrew in view of his traumatic life history, his retarded functioning, and the neurotic conflicts that were apparent. My colleague referred him to me since she knew that I was looking for an analytic case, and, after seeing Andrew and his adoptive parents a few times, I endorsed my colleague's view that he needed at least four sessions a week in order for us to have a chance to reach and work through the deepest layers of his traumatic experiences and to tackle the omnipotent defences that he had built up to cope with his feelings of abandonment and depression.

The parents agreed, and they shared the task of bringing Andrew to his sessions. I was very content and excited because it was to be my first child analysis since my move from

London to Hamburg. We had a good start, Andrew developing a strong treatment alliance and bringing a lot of material which reflected his unresolved conflicts, his regressive tendencies, and above all his identifications with invulnerable television heroes which helped him to deny how much he had been hurt and was suffering underneath. So I felt that analysis was proceeding well, that the transference was gaining in intensity, and that the analytic process was deepening.

Some months after the beginning of Andrew's analysis, his father announced in a meeting with the parents, which took place regularly every fortnight, that he had decided to move away from Hamburg to a town that was over an hour's drive away. It meant that he would no longer be able to share in bringing Andrew to some of his sessions. The mother, who was working as a teacher, was adamant that she could not bring him four times a week. No amount of persuasion and interpretation on my part helped to change her mind, so that I very reluctantly had to agree to reduce Andrew's sessions to three a week. I was sadly aware that something was repeating itself here, that Andrew was again the loser, not only having less contact with his father but also losing a quarter of his time with me.

In retrospect, I think that this change in the setting affected me more profoundly than I was aware of at the time. Andrew's treatment somehow was not the same for me any more. In quite a subtle and unconscious way, I must have withdrawn some of my emotional investment in him and his treatment. I am fairly certain that this was part of the reason why it became less productive, why it lost some of the momentum that it had gained during the first nine months, and why progress became slower. It goes without saying that my countertransference reactions to his parents who had spoiled my first analysis also played a significant part in this. These countertransference responses to parents, which affect all of us who work with children and parents at the same time, always complicate matters and demand our particular vigilance and attention.

I would now like to turn to the most difficult part of this presentation, namely, that which concerns the so-called "psychoanalytic process". It is a concept that is used a great deal these days, and we all seem to have some vague idea what we mean by it when we are using it. And yet its precise meaning remains somewhat elusive. What seems clear is that it must refer to a mental process that is the result of the special setting and conditions that characterize psychoanalysis. Thus, it must have something to do with our professional attitude and our special ways of responding to a patient's communications with our technical tools of interpretation, clarification, and confrontation. But it must also have something to do with the reliability of our presence and the undivided attention that we pay to our patients' communications.

But is it a process that occurs in the patient or in us, or is it rather something that takes place *between* the patient and his analyst, a joint product, so to speak? To my mind, the psychoanalytic process is something that does evolve in the intermediate space between analyst and patient—that it is something to which both contribute, the patient through the unfolding of his transferences and resistances, the analyst through her countertransference reactions, her understanding of the unconscious significance of the patient's material and his interpretative activity. It is the interaction of these various activities or responses that sets in motion processes in both patient and analyst that promote an ever-deepening understanding of the sources of the patient's conflicts, his defensive adaptations, his emotional economy, his healthy versus his pathological narcissism, the dynamics between his id, ego, and superego functioning, and so forth.

I think there are three main factors that have a bearing on the development of the psychoanalytic process and on its nature. One comes from the side of the patient—namely, the degree of his motivation, not only to get rid of his symptoms and to find relief for his suffering, but also a genuine wish to get to know himself better, to gain insight into the unconscious contributions to his ways of functioning and relating.

Now, we all know that this element of motivation is often lacking in children, at least at the beginning of the treatment and when they are still rather young. This does militate against the development of an effective psychoanalytic process or one that will reach great depths, although it happens not infrequently that a greater degree of motivation makes its appearance in the course of a treatment, especially if a child somehow feels helped by the treatment. In such cases, one notices that the analytic process gains momentum and reaches deeper levels of understanding.

A second main factor comes from the side of the therapist. It is related to her capacity to maintain a positive transference onto her patient in spite of negative countertransference reactions in the course of treatment. In other words, I do not believe that we can treat a patient successfully—that is, get a fruitful psychoanalytic process going—if our first encounters with the patient prior to the beginning of treatment do not elicit some positive fantasies about this patient in us, some libidinal investment, including hope. If such feeling responses are lacking in us, we are likely to run into trouble when confronted by the patient's negative transferences, which are likely to provoke similar countertransference reactions. This may in turn interfere with our ability to fuel the analytic process and keep it going.

The third main factor is extraneous to both therapist and patient since it has to do with the chosen setting, or, more precisely, with the frequency of the sessions. There is no doubt that in the majority of cases of psychoanalytical treatment some kind of process is set in motion, whatever the chosen setting. I have conducted at least one once-weekly psychotherapy where I was amazed at the depth of the analytical process that was set in motion. This happened with an extremely motivated adolescent girl who did a great deal of self-analytical work between our weekly sessions. But it is my impression, nevertheless, that such cases are exceptional.

By and large, I think that the higher the frequency of the sessions, the greater are the chances that an analytical process is set in motion which reaches deep into the patient's unconscious and which promises to lead to lasting internal changes. This has to do with factors that I have mentioned already—above all, the space and proximity in time that the high-frequency setting permits for the elaboration of fantasies on the side of both patient and analyst, the increased opportunity it provides the analyst with, both to get in touch with and understand her patient's unconscious mind, and, last but not least, the intensification and deepening of the transference and countertransference.

Although it does not specifically refer to the psychoanalytic process itself, I would like to quote a passage from Anna Freud's comments on the choice of setting which she made when, some sixteen years ago, we discussed with her the treatment situation and technique with children:

> Five times a week is the desirable number of attendances for child analysis, and even five hours weekly represents a relatively slight contact with a child. The most intensive contact feasible is needed, not only to gather the maximum amount of material, but also to keep the interpretative work going, to keep the analytic material as far as possible within the bounds of the treatment situation, to deal with the anxieties aroused by it and not to place too great a burden on the child's environment. Any lessening of the frequency of attendance for these reasons is detrimental to the efficiency of the analyst's work. [quoted in Sandler, Kennedy, & Tyson, 1980, p. 7]

Of the factors enlisted by Anna Freud in justification of a high-frequency setting, I would like to pick out only two in this context, because they are particularly relevant in terms of the psychoanalytic process: (1) the large amount of material that can be collected in this way, and (2) the upkeep of the flow of interpretation. Both of them, it seems to me, are instrumental in fostering the analytical process, the first because the wealth of material that gets accumulated in frequent contacts improves the analyst's possibilities to understand what is going on in the internal world of a child, and the second because the flow of interpretation is likely to move things in a child more rapidly and consistently than is the case in a low-frequency treatment.

Another factor that has to be taken into account in the interplay between transference, countertransference, the psychoanalytic process, and the session frequency is the kind of disturbance that one is dealing with. Most generally, I would say that low-frequency therapy can always be considered when a child's disturbance is clearly of a neurotic kind. But with severer

kinds of disturbances, such as borderline pathologies, psychoses, or autistic disturbances, it is questionable whether a low
frequency is sufficient to provide the setting necessary for the
establishment of a meaningful relationship between child and
therapist in which such a child can feel contained and held, and
in which the therapist has enough time and space to feel her way
to the child's inner world, all the more difficult because it is so
chaotic and far removed from our ordinary experiences and
functioning.

I recently had the pleasure of reading and reviewing *Live
Company* by Anne Alvarez (1992), who has such a profound
knowledge about the difficult work with such very disturbed
children. I would like to address one aspect of her long treatment
of Robbie, an autistic boy, because it is relevant to the issues I
am discussing in this presentation.

For a number of external reasons, Robbie's therapy with
Anne Alvarez started, when he was 7 years old, on a once-a-week
basis, which, at a later point, had to be reduced even to once a
month. It was only when he was 13 that he could be offered five
sessions a week. Anne Alvarez comments as follows on this
change and the reasons for it:

> His fears, his distress and anguish over any separation, from
> them [his parents] or me, his sexual mischievousness with
> women friends of theirs were overflowing even his parents'
> tolerant boundaries, and could certainly not be contained in
> once-a-month treatment. . . . The change to 5 times weekly
> treatment provided a much stronger and firmer holding situ-
> ation. Robbie's mother reported that, for the first time in his
> life, he was sleeping through the night, and not needing to be
> under about 10 blankets. [Alvarez, 1992, p. 32]

In her chapter on "Reclamation and Live Company", Alvarez
(1992) notes that "there is no doubt that my most obvious
reclamatory move—the increase to 5 times weekly treatment—
played a considerable part in the awakening process" (p. 65) and,
I would like to add, in the generation of what might be called a
psychoanalytic process in which patient and analyst become
more tuned to each other.

It is, of course, idle to speculate what might have happened if
Robbie had had the benefit of a full analysis from a younger age

onwards. But Alvarez' descriptions of the enormous difficulties one is confronted with when working analytically with such children, both in understanding and reaching them, and also as regards the vigilance about one's countertransference responses, leave no doubt in my mind that in such cases only the highest possible frequency offers the prospect of some success.

In conclusion, I want to say something about what seems to me one of the main differences between high-frequency and low-frequency treatments of neurotic children. It has to do with the question of what we are aiming for, what goals we set ourselves. I think we have no choice but to limit the goals when we see a child only once or twice a week. It is evident that in such a setting the limited time at our disposal to explore the mutual relationship between a child and us and to get familiar with the inner world of such a child, especially its more hidden unconscious parts, also puts certain limitations on what we can achieve, on how far we are able to help a child resolve existing conflicts, modify defensive organizations, or bring about changes affecting the relations between the psychic structures. I think that in the case of Andrew, whom I mentioned earlier in this chapter, I was reluctant or unable to accept that I had to change my goals once his sessions had been reduced to three and later on even to two per week.

I am fully aware that, on many occasions and in many countries, external circumstances of one kind or another are such that what we may regard as the optimal setting for the treatment of a particular child is not possible. This does not mean, however, that we cannot help that child considerably with his problems and suffering, by the application of a psychotherapeutic setting.

CHAPTER FOUR

Some problems in transference and countertransference in child and adolescent analysis

Anne-Marie Sandler

I n this chaper it will be possible to do justice to only a very small part of this crucial area of psychoanalytic psycho- therapy. The topic is essentially a clinical and technical one, rather than a theoretical one, and the analysis of the transfer- ence and the understanding of countertransference are central elements in the analysis of both adults and children. However, the concepts of transference and countertransference have changed over the years, and I want to give a very brief theoretical introduction before going on to focus on one or two of the prob- lems that arise in connection with transference interpretations and, to a certain extent, to comment on the relevant counter- transference reactions.

Although for many years—and this is still very much the case at present—transference was seen as being a repetition of past relationships to important figures in the child's life (Fenichel, 1945), we have come to realize more and more that the repetition of the past does not mean that the child or adult recreates relationships exactly as they were in the earliest years. We know that what tends to get reproduced in the present are relation- ships that have been distorted—sometimes grossly distorted—

during the course of development by the child's fantasies, by his use of mechanisms of defence such as projection and externalization.

This has led, in recent years, to the formulation that transference includes an externalization of internal object relationships. Of course, such internal relationships are based upon the child's experience of interaction with the important figures of his childhood, but the way they are established in the mind may make them far removed from the reality of the original figures. What is externalized may be a direct reflection of a fantasy derived from the internal relationship, but it may also be modified by defence. So, in two of the cases I describe here, the underlying unconscious transference wish was, I believe, a strong wish for affectionate contact with an idealized maternal object, yet the conflict this aroused resulted in a defensive withdrawal from emotional contact with the analyst and the creation of a barrier that led to the failure of the analysis.

Of course, transference manifestations, as we see them in the analysis, also occur in regard to important figures in the individual's life outside the analysis. This is particularly the case with children, where the (in many ways most appropriate) figures for transference fantasies are in fact the *parents* of the patient. If we look at the relationship of children to their parents, we can often discern what are essentially unconscious transference fantasies based on their previously created internal object relationships, fantasies that get enacted and actualized in the relationship to the parents (Sandler et al., 1980).

Just a word about countertransference: so much has been written about this topic in recent years that I shall restrict myself to saying that we can view countertransference as relating to those responses in the analyst's mind that arise in interaction with the patient, with his analytic material, and in the transference relationship. And, as we all know nowadays, the awareness of our own responses and attitudes to the patient can be (but need not necessarily be) an aid to understanding what is going on in the transference relationship. A countertransference response may arise as a result of the role the patient is forcing onto the analyst, and, especially in child analysis, the analyst may not become aware of having responded to the role until some countertransference acting out has occurred (Heimann, 1950; Orr, 1954).

Let me now turn to the cases I should like to discuss. The first of these is a boy, Jonathan*, who did well in analysis. The two cases that then follow, Carole and Mary, did not do well at all, because of an intractable transference resistance that prevented the development of a treatment alliance.

Jonathan

Jonathan, aged 6, had presented problems since birth, and the present crisis was precipitated by his having suddenly and viciously attacked his female teacher, screaming and biting her. From the interview with the parents, it appeared that Jonathan had been a source of continual anxiety, with mother convinced that he was physically damaged in some way. The parents seemed unable to set limits or agree on how to handle him. In his infancy he had been breast-fed for the first months, but was abruptly weaned when Mother was ill with severe asthma. In some ways he was a perfectionist, but at the same time he tended to regress to infantile behaviour. Father's method of controlling him was through cajoling and bribery, while Mother tended to get provoked, followed by extreme guilt. Both Father's and Mother's ways of relating to Jonathan fostered a strong tendency on his part to enter into sado-masochistic interactions.

A brother, David, was born when Jonathan was 4. David was Mother's favourite, and Jonathan was extremely jealous. At school Jonathan was a good pupil, and so his outburst towards the teacher came as a complete surprise.

Jonathan was offered treatment with an experienced therapist, Mrs N, whose work I arranged to supervise once a week. Mrs N reported that in her first session with Jonathan she had been quite taken aback by his appearance. He was small, wore large, thick spectacles, had a pinched face, and had a

---

*A slightly different version of this clinical case appeared in the *Journal of Psychotherapy*, *11* (1985).

very noticeable squint. He did not respond to Mrs N's greeting, avoided eye contact throughout the session, remaining sullen, and hid behind his mother for quite a while at the beginning of the session.

Jonathan had started to kick Mother on the way to the consulting-room, and he continued this inside the room. At first Mother tried to ignore this, but it got worse. The therapist suggested to Jonathan that he inspect the toys in the room. This had no effect, and Mrs N then commented that Mother might like to look at the toys with Jonathan. This seemed to work, and Jonathan inspected the toys, without any change of expression. He did not play until he had found a gun which shot a stick with a suction pad at the end. He then shot it all over the place and finally managed to hit Mrs N. Mrs N said that while it was fun to play with guns she didn't like to be hit, just as he would not like to be hit. She suggested that he find a target to shoot at. Jonathan accepted this, and found a small doll's house that he placed in the sandbox, using it as his target.

After Jonathan shot several times at the doll's house, he became very excited, saying, "I'll destroy you", "I'll break it all up". He managed to raise clouds of sand but then looked for something that would serve as a fortification to protect the house. He first used fences, which he blew up, shrieking with excitement and passing wind. He then found a large elephant, which he placed in front of the house. This time no amount of shooting could move the elephant. Jonathan became furious, shouting at the elephant that it was arrogant, impertinent, and that he would destroy him and teach him a lesson. "I'll show you, I'll show you", he screamed. Jonathan, in his excitement, now began to throw handfuls of sand and toys about the room.

Mrs N commented at this point, which was towards the end of the session, that she understood that Jonathan felt furious and humiliated that the elephant was so strong, because that made him feel rather small and weak, not only in the eyes of the therapist and Mother, but also in his own eyes. Jonathan did not react to this openly, but quietened down, although he went on shooting viciously at the elephant's belly.

I should like to make a few remarks about this material. It is worth noting that at the beginning of this session Mrs N orientated herself to the child's aggression and deflected it to a more neutral object by setting limits—that is, by suggesting that he find a target to shoot at. My own inclination would have been to take a different approach, as I saw the child's aggressive behaviour as motivated by anxiety, and would have tried to find some way of saying to Jonathan, either directly or via his mother, that to come to see a strange lady is perhaps very scary, and that Jonathan wants to be the one who does the scaring. Mrs N and I were able to discuss this at our regular meeting, and returned to this topic many times—and I shall also return to it here.

It seems crucial, in a patient like Jonathan, to decide whether one is faced with an impulsive, aggressive, violent child, whose ego is unable to control outbursts of rage, or whether one is dealing with an essentially *anxious* child, who is frightened because he has externalized an aggressive introject (or we can say an "aggressive internal object") in the transference, and who then deals with his unconscious transference fear by identifying with the perceived therapist/aggressor. In Jonathan's case, I had the impression that he *was* basically very frightened of the therapist and the therapeutic situation, and that his anger was a defensive reaction to having been brought to the unfamiliar and anxiety-provoking treatment situation. Mrs N was right, of course, that Jonathan was very frustrated and humiliated because the elephant's resistance emphasized to Jonathan his own weakness. But, for me, the critical point was not Jonathan's aggression and aggressive fantasies as such, but rather that he was expecting to be told that he was arrogant and full of himself and would be taught a lesson and punished. Accordingly, an interpretation of the child's fear could, in my view, have appropriately been made in the transference.

Jonathan's choice of the elephant to shoot at had, in my opinion, a clear transference implication. I thought it was a way of actually reassuring himself that the therapist would be immune to his aggression. At the same time, he could feel safer in expressing his aggression, which he had felt might get out of control. His threats to the elephant that he would destroy him and teach him a lesson seem clearly to represent Jonathan's identification with what he expected as a retaliation from the therapist. Here, again, we see evidence of the way in which the frightening introject or internal object is shown in the transference by externalization onto the person of the therapist, and then dealt with by identification with the aggressor.

That Mrs N was seen as a terrifying aggressor is borne out by a drawing that Jonathan made in his next session. It depicted a terrible monster, with human features, with many limbs and sharp teeth. But what was very striking is that inside the monster's belly Jonathan drew a clock, with the hands pointing to ten minutes before the hour. He referred to the clock, which marked off the fifty minutes of the session, as a bomb!

It took Jonathan some weeks to separate from Mother in the sessions, and in the next months Jonathan directed the sessions completely by insisting that he and Mrs N play football all the time. He would come in like a tornado, carrying his own football, neither greeting nor looking at Mrs N, and would immediately clear a space for the game. He would proceed to show Mrs N how proficient he was at kicking and dribbling the ball. He constantly tried to teach her in a very didactic way.

A few words about the football game might be appropriate. Mrs N felt that it had a most controlling quality, and showed Jonathan's need to maintain his illusion of omnipotence. He did not allow Mrs N to speak, except to indicate that she had understood his commands and instructions. There was a clear sado-masochistic element in his play, and the therapist became aware of her own countertransference urge to respond in an aggressive way to his taunts and provocations. At one point, she felt a strong impulse to defeat him in the game in order to teach him a lesson, and she then felt guilty about this. This countertransference response led us to reflect on the passivity and helplessness of Jonathan's parents, on the one hand, and on his father's sado-masochism in the endless discussions and bribery that he used to manipulate Jonathan. We both felt that the parents' inability to set limits and to control him properly tended to confirm Jonathan's fear of his own violence and destructiveness. Our understanding of this allowed Mrs N to insist that the obsessive and repetitive football game had to be checked, and that the last twenty minutes or so of the session should be spent more quietly. Jonathan accepted this, and they started to play board games — draughts, snakes and ladders, and chess. Here, again, Jonathan, as might be expected, was constantly critical and scornful of Mrs N, and he would interrupt the game when there was any danger of losing.

> Jonathan gradually become able to call his therapist by her name and to make eye contact with her. The football game became less compulsive, and it was replaced by the enactment of endless battles involving toy cars, animals, soldiers, and space invaders. Mrs N was invariably the enemy, and the conflict was always over the possession of territory. Mrs N was always the loser, and a negotiated peace was never possible. The therapist understood this material as an expression of Jonathan's reaction to his fear of being rejected, abandoned, and forgotten. His need to regain his territory and to be in charge was very evident. It is interesting that, at this point, the therapist realized that she felt unduly anxious before and during Jonathan's sessions. This anxiety disappeared when she realized that this reaction on her part was essentially a reflection of Jonathan's internal persecutory feelings, which were resonating in her.

> During the first year of the therapy, Mrs N was gradually able to create a climate in which Jonathan felt safe enough to express, in many varied ways, his rich—even though terrifying—fantasy life. At home, an improvement in Jonathan's general behaviour was reported, and all seemed well at school.

> However, Jonathan began to show signs of increasing upset at weekends and holidays. He would be aggressive towards Mrs N, yet deny that he cared about her or the separations in any way. At these times the ending of the session was clearly seen by him as an attack, a cruel reminder of his vulnerability and weakness. Mrs N had become aware that Jonathan's aggression and his provocations were aimed at controlling and immobilizing her. She felt that he wanted to have her full and constant attention, and that he feared he might be ignored and forgotten. On one occasion during this period,

Jonathan saw Mrs N in the street outside the clinic with a
small child. He refused to discuss the incident in the next
session, threatening to leave if she went on talking about
such silly matters. (I should add that normally Jonathan did
not see any of Mrs N's other patients before or after his
session.)

In the following session, which was the last of the week
Jonathan simply refused to leave. When Mrs N insisted that
the time was up, he threw about everything in the room that
he could lay his hands on, making a considerable amount of
noise in the process. Father, who heard this going on, came
to the consulting-room and was horrified to see the mess. He
insisted that he and Jonathan clear the room up. Jonathan
then left without saying goodbye, and Mrs N felt that he was
profoundly humiliated. She was quite sure that, on the way
home, Father was going to lecture Jonathan on his behaviour, even though she had repeatedly told the father that
what happens in the consulting-room concerns only Jonathan and herself.

When Mrs N saw Jonathan on the following Monday, after the
weekend break, he entered the room like a wild beast, without greeting her. He rushed to kick her and accused her of
not having got the room ready for him. He then attacked her
further, trying to bite her and scratching her face, drawing
blood. Mrs N had no choice but to hold him down while trying
to talk to him. She said to him: "Today you are very angry
and if you can talk about it that would be quite all right, but I
cannot let you hurt me." Jonathan started to scream to drown
N's voice, and struggled to get free. After a while the commo-
tion brought the Mother to the office, and both Mother and
Mrs N held Jonathan down, trying to calm him. In his struggle to get free, he knocked his lip against a piece of furniture
and it started to bleed. Jonathan did not want to leave the
session, and the struggle to stop him attacking Mrs N and
Mother continued for much of the session, ending with
Mother bribing Jonathan with the promise of a treat. He then
rushed out of the room.

Certainly Mrs N's comment to Jonathan that he was very
angry was a correct one. However, whereas Mrs N still saw

Jonathan's behaviour as an outburst of aggression which could not be contained, my own view of it was much more that it was a direct result of Jonathan's shame, guilt, and humiliation that had been stimulated in the previous session. Jonathan certainly behaved very aggressively, but it was, to my mind, due to his outrage at having been betrayed—as he thought—by the therapist, both by her apparently preferring another child to him and allowing the father to humiliate him in front of her, and by abandoning him over the weekend. We can also assume that he felt terrified after the weekend break because of a fantasy that he might be rejected and punished for his behaviour when he came to the session. So he became the aggressor engaged in a sado-masochistic struggle in which both the object and Jonathan himself were attacked.

What I have been referring to throughout this account is Jonathan's way of dealing with internal feelings of criticism by simultaneously externalizing what he felt to be the criticized part of himself—he accused Mrs N of not getting the room ready when he had felt acutely guilty about disrupting it—and identifying with what he felt to be an aggressive and sadistically humiliating superego introject. This is the mechanism of identification with the *internal* aggressor. This very common mechanism provides a double gain. The child can get rid of the guilty or shameful aspects of his own self by projection while simultaneously identifying with a powerful and frightening internal figure. My own inclination would have been to interpret consistently how he was trying to do to the therapist exactly what he feared would be done by her to him.

I have presented this case, obviously very incompletely, for a particular purpose and have not gone into any detail about Jonathan's pathology. Certainly, his early experiences played a significant part, as did the parents' externalization onto him of unwanted aspects of themselves during the course of his development. Of particular importance was his mother's pregnancy and David's birth. In all of this, his intense anger—which was not at that time defensive anger of the sort I have just been talking about—caused his fantasy life to be very violent indeed and brought about the internalization of a most harsh and critical superego. Analysis allowed him to find new solutions to his

internal conflict. However, I want to stress that this was a consequence of his having allowed himself to establish a treatment
alliance with his therapist. By the capacity for a treatment alliance in this context, I mean the capacity to mobilize internal
forces that were sufficient to counter the resistances that arose
during the course of therapy.

As a final remark about this vignette, I would like to name
some of the various countertransference aspects that can be seen
in the interaction between Jonathan and Mrs N. The first encounter is always important, and Mrs N acknowledges that she had a
negative reaction at first seeing Jonathan. Consciously, of
course, this does not affect Mrs N's professional stance, and yet
we must take notice of these countertransference feelings as they
will affect the therapist's unconscious reactions in the course of
the treatment if simply ignored. We must also assume that
Jonathan's aggressive behaviour created in the therapist a set of
feelings and fantasies, some having to do with the person of the
therapist and some with the projection of the patient. The awareness and sorting out of these reactions would allow for better
understanding of the patient's communications. In this vignette,
one could perhaps say that Mrs N's countertransference made it
difficult for her at times to differentiate between destructiveness
and anxiety when faced with Jonathan's wild and uncontrolled
behaviour. At other times, her capacity to be firm in setting limits
and to avoid being drawn into masochistic battles showed that
she was not enmeshed in unanalysed countertransference conflicts. Finally, when Mrs N realized how anxious she felt before
and during some of Jonathan's sessions, she could use these
countertransference feelings to understand the feelings, anxieties, and fantasies of the child and better interpret what was
going on.

Carole

I should now like to address a very different problem. At the
Anna Freud Centre we have for many years been concerned
about a small number of children who come to therapy but do
not appear to gain much, or indeed any, benefit from it. The
cases I am referring to have been carefully assessed, as all our
therapy cases are, but although they were regarded as suitable
for therapy, they never appeared to settle into a satisfactory

analytic relationship. We have found that therapists tend to go on seeing these children, hoping for a change, which does not in fact materialize. The therapist may be faced with a withdrawn, passive, at times hostile child who does not seem able to cooperate in any attempt at the therapeutic work.

I want to speak of the case of Carole, who was 11 when she started analysis and 12½ when it was terminated. Her treatment was conducted by a young colleague, who described how the analysis failed because interpretations hardly ever penetrated the massively defensive personality structure.

Carole had a background of great instability, with her father leaving and subsequently marrying again when Carole was 5. A little later her mother moved, taking Carole and her three older sisters and a new husband. They settled in a small village, where the mother opened a general store. We may assume that she was rarely available to care for her children, and when Carole was 9, the mother and step-father quarrelled and, supposedly not to jeopardize the marriage further, the mother put Carole and two of her sisters on the train to their father and step-mother, telephoning the father to say that they were on their way.

The family in which Carole lives at present includes her father, a businessman who is himself the product of a broken marriage. He impressed the analyst as materially concerned but emotionally detached and determined to remain unaware of the not inconsiderable problems of his present wife and children.

The step-mother, Tessa, is a dominant, competent woman who copes with a large family, a multitude of animals, a part-time job, and much else besides. It became clear that this frantic activity was a defence against depression, and that she was a woman who could not afford to "let up" in any way. Other family members include Kate, aged 16 years, Carole's sister—a pretty, vivacious girl who despised Carole's two older sisters. One, an asthmatic, moved back to live with their mother, and the other now lives independently.

Little information was available at the diagnostic stage about Carole's personal history. It was thought that breast-feeding had been satisfactory, and it was known that toilet training had never been wholly successful. When she was sent back to her father at the age of 9, she was described as a "nervous wreck", who soiled, suffered from croup, and was unable to speak for herself at all. Father recalled as a "joke" that Carole did not know what foods she liked or disliked, what she wanted to do, whether she was tired or not. Certainly, this difficulty and confusion in expressing her own wishes and needs was still very much in evidence when she started treatment.

Carole was referred at the age of 11 to The Anna Freud Centre by the consultant psychiatrist of a local Child Guidance Clinic because he considered her to be a deeply disturbed girl who was failing so badly at her schooling that she was refusing to attend school. With a change to a less academic establishment, the school refusal disappeared, but doubt was expressed about whether she was working to her potential and about her ability to concentrate.

Associated with the school problem, Carole was stealing at school. The stealing had now spread to her home, and she was known to have stolen her step-brother's pen and watch. Her father described her stealing as "compulsive". Tessa said that she could cope with Carole's soiling, but she just could not control her anger towards Carole when she stole. Carole had been soiling constantly since she came to live with her father and step-mother three years before. As far as was known, she was also soiling prior to leaving her mother. It was clear that Carole was intensely unhappy and affectively withdrawn in her relationships with adults. Carole herself was most concerned about her "forgetting"; this symptom seemed to cover her problems of relationships with others, her inhibition of curiosity, and her inability to listen and concentrate.

While Carole's presenting symptoms are complex, possibly the most relevant from the point of view of our discussion today has to do with her narcissistic devaluation of herself. This devaluation, this view of herself as faecal, dirty, and rejectable, was central to her underlying pathology and was possibly one of the main deterrents to the establishment of a treatment alliance. She simply could not envisage herself as having any importance for the analyst or for anyone else. This view of Carole was implicit in the referral symptoms and in what the father and step-mother said of her at the diagnostic stage. I would suggest that a narcissistic defect of this order has to be set against the child's possible capacity to form a treatment alliance and to work within an analytic relationship. But how can we judge this initially? Do we take into account the real-life experiences of the child, and do these experiences have to be at least minimally gratifying? Or does the child have at least to have maintained a hopeful fantasy that future experiences and future relationships will prove to be better than the real ones of the past and the present?

Against the back-cloth of her life experiences, Carole would be justifiably doubtful and mistrustful of the genuineness of the help that the analyst offered her. One would expect her to question and to be continually suspicious of the analyst's motives, but, in the event, Carole did everything she could to keep any awareness of her unhappiness out of consciousness, and she was single-minded in directing her efforts against the analyst's attempts to verbalize and explore her feelings. Such attempts presented a dangerously disruptive threat to whatever adaptive and relatively safer inner balance she had managed to establish, and she wanted none of it; she quite simply did not wish to be in touch with any painful affective states.

Mary

Carole's story strongly reflects an experience I had some years ago of therapy with a 17-year-old girl, whom I shall call Mary, and who was in treatment for over a year before suddenly terminating.

Mary also came from a broken family. Her father was an alcoholic, on most days coming home drunk. He was not aggressive, nor was he violent, but would be intrusively maudlin and exhibitionistic. The father left her mother when Mary was 5, and the mother has worked ever since to support the family. As far as Mary could remember, her mother had always been consistently busy, not only working in the daytime, but in the evenings as well, leaving Mary and her brother, three years older, in the care of a neighbour. Mary was referred to me for therapy because of failure at school. She was still at school but had a block or—one could say—an inhibition in learning. She was accident-prone, and her relationships with the other children at school were superficial; she often changed friends.

When I first saw Mary she appeared to welcome the opportunity to see someone for help. At our first encounter, I was struck by her appearance—she looked much younger than her age, like a mouse, shy and effacing, hapless and grey. She seemed very anxious, but soon started to cry, silently letting tears trickle down her cheeks. She was reluctant to speak, but relaxed when I mentioned that it was understandably difficult to talk to a stranger and that it might be frightening to come to an unknown place to see someone she did not know. She managed to compose herself and to make fleeting eye contact. When I asked if she could tell me a little about herself, she spoke rather hesitantly about her mother and brother in a somewhat idealized and glamourized way. When I tried to find out something about herself, she said that she had nothing to add.

At first I understood this behaviour to be an extreme form of shyness, expecting her to be more confident with time, and I felt protective and warm towards her. As the therapy progressed, however, Mary's refusal to speak, or even to look at me, took on a stubborn quality which at times left me exasperated. I was forced to rely to a large extent on my countertransference feelings, and my interpretations—however tentative—nearly always received no response from Mary. Sometimes I caught a glimpse of acknowledgement; at other times she reacted with a small triumphant smile. But for the most part, she seemed to resent being with me and annoyed that she was expected to cooperate. She was on occasion able to acknowledge that she felt suspicious of my motives, and she said that she did not understand why I wanted to see her, except perhaps to earn money. She clearly felt criticized when I tried to address what I saw as her problems or her unhappiness. I was fairly sure that Mary was, among other things, having to battle with her homosexual impulses in the transference, but there was no way in which I was able to approach the subject successfully with her.

It would be easy to say that the fact that Mary kept on coming fairly regularly was an indication of her wish to be helped, and to say that her passive aggression should have been properly interpreted. In fact it became clearer, as time went on, that Mary used the fact that she was in therapy to cover her failure at school—to testify that she was ill and should not be blamed. Finally, she removed herself from treatment at a time when she was about to leave school, having failed her examinations.

* * *

You may well ask why it is that I have presented the cases of Carole and Mary, in which the treatment had failed. I have done this because both these children pose us a puzzling problem. It is possible to say, as Carole's therapist did, that these children do not establish a treatment alliance, but this seems to me to beg the question. We have to ask: why don't they improve? I can only give you my impression, which is that the attitude of the child in the therapy reflects a transference from the relationship with the primary object to the person of the therapist, a transference that is so immediate and so concrete that there is no room for elaboration, no capacity in the child to think or conceive of alternatives. So one can postulate a paucity of adequate defences, an impoverishment of the child's fantasy life, with a tremendous need to control any urge or wish to relate more closely, because of an overwhelming fear of disappointment. Although Mary was adolescent, and her wish for closeness appeared to be mixed with homosexual strivings, it seems likely that the same process of defence and ego constriction was at the root of both Carole's and Mary's learning problems. While in both cases this defensive constriction, which showed itself as resistance in the analysis, was clearly understood, any interpretation of it had no impact on the girls, except to cause further withdrawal.

In children of this sort, it seems to me that the affect of shame is central to their sense of self. As a consequence, they feel worthless, hopeless, valueless, as if they were some kind of unwanted garbage. In turn, they have to denigrate and frustrate the object by not, so-to-speak, giving of themselves. In this way, they also protect themselves from exposing what they regard as the bad and inferior aspects of themselves. What they defend against so strongly in therapy is the threat of developing a positive, trusting, even affectionate transference to the therapist. One cannot help being reminded here of the importance of what Phyllis Greenacre has called the "basic" or "primary" transference, which she regards as originating in a primary need for sensory contact with the mother, for the warmth of contact with another body (Greenacre, 1954). Winnicott's formulation of what he has described as "good-enough mothering", and the importance of the shared experience of interacting in a free and safe way in the play between infant and mother, can be considered as an extension of Greenacre's idea. Winnicott has stressed—in my view quite correctly—that it is this early play that facilities the individual's growth and social relationships, and it is, in a sense, the capacity for play which is the essence of the relationship between patient and therapist. The incapacity to create a psychic space for play in therapy is, I believe, largely a consequence of the need of these children to protect themselves from yearnings for closeness to the object, yearnings that are highly threatening to them (Winnicott, 1965).

It might be interesting to consider that patients like Carole and Mary have, in a sense, tremendous fear of regressing towards a very early mode of gratification in their object relationship, a type of close relationship with the object which they unconsciously yearn for but in no way can permit. They cannot let go of what appears to us to be an unsatisfactory mode of coping but is for them the safest posture to take up, lest they become engulfed by primitive urges that could not be managed and would lead to inevitable and overwhelming disappointment.

In these kinds of cases, the countertransference reactions can be very powerful and difficult to acknowledge and cope with. To be repeatedly de-skilled is both painful and hurtful, and if this goes unnoticed and unchecked it can lead to unconscious enactment. I have sometimes wondered whether the tendency to go on for years with a treatment like Mary's and Carole's could sometimes be due to our own blind spots which make it so difficult to conceive that what we offer may not be the treatment of choice.

I should like to say, in conclusion, that there are a great many sources of difficulty in handling and interpreting the transference in our work with children and adolescents, and I am conscious of having only touched on the subject. I am also aware that there was much more that could have been said about the countertransference—in particular, as in the treatment of adolescent patients in which the whole issue of sexuality can present both the patient and the therapist with a wide variety of transference and countertransference difficulties. However, in this chapter I have restricted myself to the presentation of material from three cases which presented special problems in the transference and countertransference factors affecting the treatment alliance.

CHAPTER FIVE

The transference mirage and the pitfalls of countertransference (with special emphasis on adolescence)

François Ladame

Introduction

According to Freud, transference emerges from unresolved unconscious conflict. Treating neurotic persons analytically means being able to analyse *the* transference. From there, we progressively moved to the idea that transference results from the analytic situation itself (analysis then is defined as analysis *within* the transference). Can we move yet one step further and view its beginning within the proposition of analysis itself, which means a move towards reopening closure that was necessary for the subject's constitution?

At first despised, countertransference has become more and more prized, until now being recognized as the central tool of the dynamics of the analytical process: a meeting of the unconscious within itself. From one extreme to the other.

Certain characteristics of the adolescent process, which give specific flavour to both transference and countertransference with adolescent patients, are also underlined in this chapter.

* * *

For a comprehensive grasp of the phenomena of transference, I recommend the recent paper by Abend (1993). I limit myself here to one particular viewpoint, though I want nevertheless to emphasize some of Abend's warnings regarding today's divergences with which I fully agree: the current interest in sexual abuse leads to the overlooking of the central importance of conscious and unconscious infantile sexual theories, wishes, and fears, and their effect on transference. Theories of transference that are derived mainly from work with severely disturbed patients—as well as from a particular emphasis on non-verbal communication—should at least elicit reservations.

Let me now go on and explain the first part of my chapter's title: "The Transference Mirage". A patient of mine, in her early 20s, tells me about a short dream: "*An adolescent girl is lying down. She tells someone: 'Shall we go and visit the Temple of the Sun?'*"

Who is "someone"? Who is she? Who is the temple? What I mean by "the transference mirage" is the paradox whereby the subject needs the other (the analyst) to visit the (her own) temple—that is, needs the other's speculum to look at her own inner world (body), but at the same time cannot but discover that there is an altar in the Temple (of the sun), which means that she is not what she thought she was. She (the patient) is another; the sun and the altar are already within, part of her identity. She cannot but discover that what she so fears/wishes for—the in-going speculum—has already happened: she has been appropriated—from the beginning. "I am another." The identity is scandalous. But the paradox does not limit itself to this bewildering discovery: it is also because the other is otherwise than he or she believes to be that the analysand may innocently take the analyst for someone other than she is.

With the establishment of transference, there is reopening of an earliest relationship when the other was primal to oneself. The constitution of the subject, of the I, needs closure (through primary repression, development of the agencies of the mind, "taking in" the other, and its concealment by building in the unconscious). I agree with Laplanche (1992) when he stresses that this reopening—the transference—is triggered by offering an analysis, by the offer made by the analyst, which re-enacts the original seduction. The analytic process itself and its outcome are quite another story.

This also means that we can draw a parallel between transference and adolescence: the adolescent task is to constitute an identity, an I, while at the same time discovering himself appropriated ("The Uncanny", to be understood here as transitory experiences of depersonalization). But the appropriation has to remain unrecognized; it is part of what forever has not to be known: it is part of the "enigma". The first relationship between mother and infant is woven by interlocking the threads of unconscious, forbidden desires, which can only remain as a riddle. The analytic setting restates the situation of these primary relationships.

According to Aulagnier (1988), the transferential relationship is close to (without duplicating) the relation as lived with a mother endowed with the attributes of complete knowledge and all-powerful love, which means that transference will trigger experiences of dependency in the realm of knowledge. Nevertheless, the "enigma" has to remain forever unanswered by attaining negative intentionality (Ladame, 1995) while leaving creativity of the mind.

To rephrase my views in a different way, primary identification is a central landmark (Cahn & Ladame, 1992): either it remains omni-present but unreachable, underlying the process of shared thinking without which there is no analytical process, or it impedes the process by provoking annihilating anxieties and blurring any difference in the illusion of fusion with its counterpart: an alienated identity.

* * *

To start with, countertransference was conceived by Freud (1910d) as interferences with the analyst's ability to understand her patient, which meant residual pathology within the analyst (her blind spots); hence the necessity for him to undergo a new analysis. This was indeed a long time ago, and today's acceptation generally includes the whole spectrum of the analyst's emotional reactions, which may serve and/or impede the treatment process. Such a shift means focusing, here and there, on whatever the analyst is experiencing: symptoms, emotions, prejudgements, unconscious reactions, ideals, and so on, rather than considering what the analyst triggers within the transference. We all know that Heimann (1950) initiated this trend and (along with Little, 1951, and Tower, 1956) was among the first analysts to view countertransference as a central tool in the analytic work. But to do justice to Freud, we must remember that he gave the first inkling into the direction of what we see today as the risks and pitfalls when he wrote in 1913, "I have good reasons for asserting that everyone possesses in his own unconscious an instrument with which he can interpret the utterances of the unconscious in other people" (1913i, p. 320), and two years later in 1915, "It is a very remarkable thing that the Ucs. of one human being can react upon that of another, without passing through the Cs. This deserves closer investigation, especially with a view to finding out whether preconscious activity can be excluded as playing a part in it" (1915e, p. 194). The latter remarks seem to me as the starting point of what I consider current deviations and excesses. It is as if Freud's queries about preconscious activity had been understood as a definite statement that indeed the preconscious might simply be ignored.

Rather than being centred on countertransference, I would advocate that the psychoanalyst's analytic skills rely mainly on her attentive listening to the patient's words as well as on an excellent memory. I now comment further on what I see as the pitfalls of overstressing countertransference as a unique tool.

The worst examples, and also the most significant, are those "intuitive" psychoanalysts relying only on themselves, tuned to their own and their patient's unconscious, and therefore limiting any possibility of verifying their intuitions through a detailed account of the sessions' *verbal* material. (I am not depicting imaginary colleagues. They indeed exist and ask for acknowledgement.) We must be well aware of the danger of ignoring that psychoanalysis' unique tool is language: we understand our patients when we carefully listen to them, and we influence them through our words. What I mean is that language testifies to the process of *linking* psychic forces and reflects an ability for symbolization. Treating borderline or psychotic patients, as we all do, does not imply a complete revision of our theory. What we target is to "neuroticize" the very ill patients rather than accepting borderline functioning as a standard. Therefore, we must respond to Freud's 1915 questions about the preconscious by strengthening its central activity and role. This would mean not accepting a theory of simple communication between *two* unconsciouses, because the latter would mean disgarding the central function of repression. We need to *mediate* when confronted with the potential trauma of the "enigma". Reopening the past must proceed step by step because past closure meant that what might have been and might now be known should not be known (parental sexuality belongs forever to the realm of what has to remain unknown). The point is that borderline patients indeed lack that kind of mediation. "Closure" is still uncertain, and they always revolt and refuse to submit to this unavoidable human law (because it would mean too strong a regressive pull towards complete powerlessness and undifferentiation). The patients' permanent stance, "one is concealing things from me", reflects, by projection, the difficulties of confronting oneself with one's own otherness, with this reality that "I am another", which is synonymous with alienated identity.

Another risk of attributing such importance to countertransference is erroneously to define mistakes in the treatment process as simply reflecting countertransference issues. This is an easy solution for teaching analysts who therefore do not have to accept failures within the teaching programme, and can also maintain the illusion that many young therapists have innate knowledge of psychopathology and interpretative work.

Were I to offer a somewhat offensive definition of countertransference, I would define it as the rationalization of the analyst's contemplation of her navel! This notwithstanding implies putting emphasis on narcissistic stances. Any time an analyst is questioned by her patient (by what the patient says or doesn't say, does or doesn't do) and feels the challenge as narcissistically frightening, I would speak of countertransference. Such reactions play against the therapeutic process insofar as an analyst who is narcissistically frightened loses all her ability to contain and mirror. Adolescent patients can be particularly expert in this kind of game, where it may well happen that either inexperienced or even experienced therapists eventually feel obviated as subjects. The therapeutic process has evolved to a point where the patient projects onto the analyst his own helplessness and fears while acting out his fantasized omnipotence, thereby reducing the analyst to an insignificant entity.

* * *

I now proceed to the third and last part of my chapter, in which I underline some characteristics of transference and countertransference with adolescent patients which are linked to the developmental process itself. I limit myself to the issues that seem to me more challenging in the treatment of sick adolescents (treatment being considered as indispensable both by patient and therapist).

The central challenge is a perverse solution (either as a risk for the future or as something that is on the way to being settled). To me this means, in reference to what I have written above, refusal of the "enigma", refusal of leaving unanswered the question, "Did she love me or did she not, while she loved someone else?", and finding one's way out of the dilemma of despising the reality of maternal love. A male patient of mine expresses it this way: "Now that I know what it means to come, it's obvious that her mother's love was only a trick; what she really loved was to fuck with Dad." Within a split transference, the patient despised the setting as well as the therapeutic process along with its rule of abstinence because he had anything he wished for outside my office (i.e. a "double" of his analyst with whom he very often was on the brink of perverse sexual acting out), hence he would think: "What else can you offer me but shit?" At the same time, he despised in a similar way what might happen with his analyst's "double" because the latter was but a poor likeness. These transferential situations are very tricky because we also have to monitor carefully where the patient is situated between a defensive transitory compromise and a more permanent perverse solution in which splitting would be "airtight", denial successful, and anxiety eradicated.

Certainly we are reassured when remembering the fragility of our patients' narcissistic resources, but it also happens that the same fragility may well be pushed to the forefront as an alibi once both analyst and patient have become aware of what is going on in the cure. This would mean that the analytic process has been successfully redirected from its usual path, and a status quo position is now preferred to one of change.

Laufer and Laufer (1989) have highlighted how the destructive impulses become an essential part of the transference relationship in the analytic work with ill adolescents. They also advise the analyst to keep constantly in mind the adolescent's hatred of the analyst for supposedly being in omnipotent control over him (p. 175).

I will paraphrase some of the different ways in which the Laufers suggest that destructive impulses can be expressed or enacted:

- The analyst is more and more aware of her own fear that actual violence might be directed at her or at others. Such a situation looks like a perverse sexual relation, in which splitting is firmly established and one's own body is no longer experienced as a persecuting enemy. The risk of resorting to a perverse solution has to be constantly monitored.
- The analyst is constantly on the alert for the possibility of self-destructive attacks. In such a situation, violence is not directed at the transference relationship but against the body itself, which means that transferential emotions are originally more repressed and internal persecution is in the foreground.
- The analyst is faced with her own feelings of helplessness or confusion (which reflect destructive attacks either against the setting itself or the analyst's capability to function as an analyst). Such a situation may be understood as a repetition of the developmental breakdown, which now looks like a transferential breakdown.

For Laufer and Laufer, the analyst's own anxiety during the treatment of such adolescents should not be considered a reflection of her "blind spots", but be understood, instead, as a predictable response to a patient whose pathology unconsciously relies on destructiveness or violence, and I agree with the Laufers on this point. According to my experience, such reactions, which can result in discouragement and acting outs by the analyst, are better dealt with in group discussions and controls than in the more classical setting of individual supervision.

Conclusion

In this chapter, I draw a parallel between transference and adolescence in that the adolescent's task is to constitute an identity whilst feeling that he is constantly at risk of facing appropriation and alienation. These anxieties date back to the time when the other was primal to oneself. Transference also brings one face to face with one's own otherness ("I am another"), and analysis exposes one to that same risk.

I also give my own views on current variations and excesses around the issue of countertransference and stress my view that the unique tool of psychoanalysis is not countertransference but language. I would speak of countertransference whenever we are challenged by our patients, especially when we feel that challenge as a narcissistic threat. This happens quite often with adolescent patients!

Finally, I underline the imperative need to monitor closely in analysis (a) the balance between helplessness and omnipotence (b) the risks of the adolescent establishing a permanent perverse solution, and (c) the importance and usefulness of the therapist monitoring her own anxiety during the treatment of very ill adolescents as a barometer of the destructiveness of the patient.

CHAPTER SIX

The influence
of the presence of parents
on the countertransference
of the child psychotherapist

Jacqueline Godfrind

Introduction

The concept of countertransference is far from unequivocal. More than any other notion relating to psychoanalytic practice, it has been marked by the development of the theory of technique. So before embarking upon the particular viewpoint that I have chosen to enlarge upon here, it seemed necessary to me to define the meaning that I am attributing to it.

I am not concerned with the history of the concept, nor with the influence of the various schools of thought upon the meanings attached to it. All I wish to do is to state briefly my personal position.

There has been an increasing interest in countertransference since Freud, who limited its application to the influence of the patient on the unconscious feelings of the therapist—an influence brought about by the patient's transference. It was understood in its negative aspect, as a generator of "blind spots" prejudicial to the analytic work and inappropriate (Freud, 1910d).

Paula Heimann's (1950) article was decisive in the widening of the concept. It will be recalled that she established its use in the regular work of the analyst, whereby the awareness of feelings and representations aroused by the patient gives access to new understanding of transference phenomena.

Today, the concept of countertransference, at least the one to which I adhere, includes the following two components of the analyst's mental functioning: that which masks the perception of some parts of the transference, and that which contributes to the understanding of the transference. The two can be integrated into a rather more general concept: countertransference can be considered as the psychic activity deployed by the analyst in response to the promptings of the analysand. It includes both conscious and unconscious reactions. But equally it engages the individuality of the analyst marked by her personal history and the theories and techniques she espouses. Every therapeutic situation, therefore, is defined by the specific transference–countertransference space that it generates.

Within this specificity the distinctive features of the therapeutic situation operate. Amongst these, the treatment of a child will introduce modifications into the therapist's countertransference. Furthermore, the treatment of a child must inevitably take the existence of the parents into account in the therapeutic process. I propose in this chapter to look at some of the interferences caused by the presence of parents in psychotherapeutic work with children.

The work of the child psychotherapist

The work of the child psychotherapist has two functions: an *interpreting* one, and a *symbolizing* one provided by a symbolizing countertransference. Both are dependent on the transference relationship. The interpreting function is aimed at the "neurotic" part of the personality and corresponds to the traditional interpretative work of understanding and interpreting the latent content of the material—making the unconscious fantasies conscious.

In my book *Les deux courants du transfert* [The Two Currents of Transference] (Godfrind, 1993), I developed the idea of "a symbolizing countertransference". Alongside the "neurotic transference" which indicates a psyche that is capable of integrating internal and external stimuli, I proposed a "basic transference" that is manifest in the more immediate reactions to the therapist. These are primary reactions such as actings out, massive affects, psychosomatic symptoms, and so forth which are indicative of a lack of introspection, in contrast to secondary reactions. In defective or psychotic children, much of the transference displays this "basic" type. In these cases, the main aim of therapy is to improve mental development. Indeed, it might be said that the therapist is *the mediator* of access to progress in the capacities for psychic integration. From the relationship that is built up between the child and the therapist—a relationship that, I think, repeats the vicissitudes of the primary relationship with the mother—I postulate some indications that may help the therapist in her interventions. In my opinion, the therapist's work unfolds on the following three axes:

- An attempt at binding. Inspired by the idea of "the mother's capacity for reverie" (Bion, 1962) or "thinking container", it consists of naming affects, conveying the meaning of acting out, creating links, etc.
- Concern with the introduction of "the Other" and with work on separation, recognizing differences, etc.
- Taking into account the necessity of a third person who will make release from the dyadic relationship possible.

Although these theoretical pointers may help guide the therapist's work, I think that nevertheless it is above all the therapist's own capacity for symbolization—that is, for transforming external promptings into psychic elements—that is the dynamic force behind what I call the symbolizing countertransference. The degree to which the therapist herself can function "symbolically" determines her ability to intervene according to whatever role falls to her: *thinking* through the transference–countertransference relationship, giving meaning to the emotional parameters of the situation, communicating her psychic working-through by linking with what is being acted and experienced, and so on. However the capacity for "thinking symbolically" is subject to eclipse by promptings that go beyond the threshold of psychic integration, and therapists are no exception to the rule. I shall come back to this. In practice, the work in question is made possible by means of the setting, the stability of which ensures the establishment of a therapeutic space.

The presence of the parents

In addition to other specific characteristics of work with children (contact through play, body involvement, etc.), the presence of the parents is one of the parameters that are liable to disrupt the therapist's functioning.

Interference from the existence of the parents is strongly in evidence from the planning stages of psychotherapeutic treatment. However, psychotherapy is only indicated for children if there is parental collaboration and agreement.

This means that from the start of therapy the presence of the parents will weigh on the therapist's countertransference. The parent's conscious attitude—but, above all, their unconscious attitude—determines the possibility of bringing a child's treatment to a successful conclusion or at least to see it through to a point dependent on their tolerance.

The evaluation of how and which unconscious resistances of the parents will later influence treatment is, as we know, difficult. How will the parents adapt to changes in the child and the self-questioning this will pose? Furthermore, how are encounters between the therapist and the parents to be managed in reality? Such questions confront the therapist from the start of therapy.

As a result, the parents' presence creates a situation that faces the therapist with the need constantly to metabolize a complex dimension—namely, the dialectic of the intersubjective and environmental in the understanding of mental functioning. I shall explain. All theorizing about psychic development must take into account the influence of the outside world on the one hand, and intrapsychic organization on the other. From Freud to the present day, questions bearing upon the respective importance of these two factors in the structuring of the mind have never ceased to fuel controversy. The oscillation between Freud's "neurotica", a theory that puts the responsibility for symptoms firmly in the external world (e.g. paternal seduction), and the theory of intrapsychic fantasies relating to psychosexuality, retains its topicality even if it is expressed in more "modern" terminology.

The presence of the parents constantly *actualizes* for the therapist the reality of environmental factors, thereby risking a biased understanding of the intrapsychic in terms of the relative weight to give to internal and external reality. This is doubtless the reason why child psychotherapy, especially, leads to a highlighting of opposing views of countertransference that sustain theoretical concepts that sometimes differ quite radically in the relative weight accorded to external trauma and intrapsychic factors.

Be that as it may, the parental presence introduces parameters liable to disrupt the therapist's functioning on the one hand through intrusions at the level of *the setting*, and on the other hand at the level *of the fantasy interactions*, both conscious and especially unconscious, that are at play between parents and therapist. The consequences of this may be manifest in the therapist in either her symbolizing or her interpreting roles. Thus one can envisage distortions of the therapist's functioning in different ways:

- *Distortions in the symbolizing qualities* of the therapist whose capacities for thinking about the situation may be affected. I am thinking of the appearance of incongruous behaviour, inappropriate emotional reactions, etc., which are the expression of momentary weaknesses in the therapist's ability to integrate psychically the promptings to which she is subjected, which are then expressed in her, too, in a regressive manner, betraying disturbances in her capacities for containing.

- *Distortions in the understanding of the fantasy contents* of the child. This may be contaminated by the therapist's apprehension of the parents' personality. But it may equally occur through the difficulty in assuming certain transference positions as a result of the way in which the therapist is affected by the parent–child relationship.

Careful consideration of factors that disrupt the therapist can lead to a deeper understanding of the mechanisms at play in the countertransference.

The effects of the setting

The importance of the fundamental *stability* of the setting requires no further proof: it is generally agreed today that it is this stability that ensures the conditions that enable the psychic capacities of the two protagonists in the therapeutic relationship to function at an optimal level:

• The setting is not only indispensable for the patient, it is equally so for the therapist, who is protected from excessive demands, and in which the symbolizing functioning is fostered as much as possible. In this perspective, two essential functions of the setting can be considered:

(a) Through its stability and permanence, the setting represents for patient *and* therapist the assurance of the *basic confidence* necessary for *thinking* in the therapeutic situation. Bleger (1967) expresses this function of the setting when he says that it immobilizes the psychotic parts of the personality, which enables the unfolding and analysis of the "healthy parts" to take place.

(b) The setting represents a "third element", making possible the *decentring* of a too-restricted dual relationship. This holds for the therapist too, the parameters of the setting enabling her to stand back somewhat from her patient to assist the therapist's psychic working-through of the situation.

• The setting is based on the existence of a *contract*, which binds therapist and patient, a contract that is deduced as the conditions for therapeutic work. It is in this that it can be said, in agreement with Donnet (1973), that there is connivance of the real and the symbolic: it is because therapist and patient have decided to be together in order to communicate *in a predetermined setting* that they can engage in this perilous adventure, this immersion in especially unconscious psychic reality. In principle, the initial contract seals an alliance that may well (but does not always) prevent excessive projective drifts and maintain the transference–countertransference relationship on a level of shared psychic working-through. This latter ability also concerns the psychic functioning of the analyst, a functioning that, as I explained earlier, defines and establishes the therapist in her role.

And for the child? Certainly some contract exists with him: "It is 'ok' to come. . . ." And indeed, as Diatkine (Diatkine & Simon, 1972) stresses, the child is particularly (perhaps rather "naively") sensitive to the therapist's interpreting function. But both of them, child and therapist, view their setting as subordinate to the good, and often bad, wishes of the parents; in the latter situation, it could be said that the setting is *perverted* by a third desymbolized party who acts against its stabilization.

Every child therapist knows about the pangs induced in therapist and child alike by parental intrusion. However, I do want to emphasize the impact that these interferences have, not only on the therapist's experience in relation to the parents, but also, and more especially, on her symbolizing capacities— sometimes the disturbance can reach the point of psychic disintegration. Actions, emotional discharges, and sometimes an incapacity to think can be the lot of the therapist subjected to misappropriation of the setting by the parents.

When the setting is broken into, therapists' reactions may take extreme and relatively conscious forms. The conscious nature of them makes control easier: rage against the parents, bitterness at their unawareness of the conditions for therapeutic work, and so on cannot be disguised in the countertransference. Unconscious reactions are, obviously, by definition, more difficult to manage. They can be detected, either through self-analysis of the countertransference, or by supervision. Two examples will illustrate my point.

A nine-year-old boy

The first is a personal example of which I retain bitter memories. It concerns the therapy of a 9-year-old boy, which had been going very well for one and a half years. Then, as sessions went by, an apathy set in which it took me some time to notice. I can see us now, him tirelessly cutting rolls of Plasticine into little slices, me abstracted, ossified, incapable of giving meaning to an impression of infinite heaviness— until I shake myself out of it and realize that I have to do something. In this case, I go and speak to the mother's therapist, as was the practice at the institution where I was working at the time, only to learn that the marriage was in a bad way, that there was a question of putting the child into boarding-school, and that the therapy was under severe threat. I realized, in listening to my colleague, that in fact, in some part of me, I had sensed this reality during earlier contacts when I was being careful not to return to denying, splitting the reality that I did not want to see with my young patient, unconsciously eroding my capacities for symbolizing the situation.

Nathalie

The other example is richer and less radical. It was observed and reported in a group supervision. Nathalie was a psychotic child treated for several years by a female therapist who carried out some fine and subtle work. Nathalie developed well. She emerged from her confused universe to communicate with her therapist at a more and more structured, represented, and symbolized level. The oedipal organization was becoming apparent: the latest sessions were devoted to pre-adolescent love affairs and drawings of clothes and jewellery. On this particular day, she arrived and drew bouquets of flowers. Her therapist was silent, perplexed. Then Nathalie drew a house, and her therapist intervened abruptly to tell her that she "was looking for a good, safe and warm breast", an interpretation that, she told us, was inspired by the shape of the roof of her house. This time it was the group that was perplexed. The interpretation seemed out of place, incongruous to us. The therapist, who was not accustomed to that kind of interpretation, agreed with us. What had happened? Her first association led her to the fact that she was at that time reading Melanie Klein with great interest . . . No one was convinced by that. Gradually, the therapist began to recall her meeting with the patient's mother, who, just before the session, had cancelled the next two sessions. The attitude of the therapist's countertransference then became clearer to us: she began the session under the blow of the news of the intended break in the setting, which provoked some degree of psychic shock; half aware of unease, she intervened in the form of action: her "interpretation" was of the "wild" kind, signifying a momentary de-symbolization of thinking in the sense of a lack of integration of the emotional and cognitive data of the therapeutic situation. The "content" of her intervention was, obviously, not "anodyne". It could be said that the counter-cathexis of her violence against the mother came out in the reference to a "good breast, safe and warm", which consoled both the young patient and her therapist against the vicissitudes imposed by a "bad external breast".

We seek consolation where we can—and seek to avoid confrontation with fantasy repercussions of the parents' presence on the interpreting function, a second form of parental interference with which I would now like to deal.

The influence of meeting with the parents on the conscious and unconscious fantasies of the therapist and their repercussion on the analytic work

The distinction I am making between these two parameters—the effects of the setting and meeting the parents—is too clear-cut. It is obvious that the two aspects overlap and interfere endlessly in the therapist's countertransference. However, there is an important difference in the mode of action on the therapist of these two parameters. *The insecurity linked to the setting*, which I have just exemplified, touches on a fundamental problem in the therapist. The interference of the parents may re-actualize the unreliability of the primordial object of the therapist by breaking the stability of the conditions of therapeutic work. This kind of breakdown in the setting arouses reactions that disturb the exercise of the elaborative (symbolizing) capacities of the therapist. However, the anxieties linked to this basic area are also transposed into *fantasies* relating to the parents: grievances about them are elaborated in fantasy scenarios, which will also have repercussions on the therapeutic work, a parameter I shall consider later.

But let us come to the meeting with the parents *in reality*, emphasizing once more that manifestations or questions at the conscious level of countertransference should not cause us to forget that the vital aspect of countertransference lies at the unconscious level and that therefore it is essential to give ourselves the means of detecting its hidden elements.

The "reality" of the child

Through meeting with the parents, the therapist gathers some elements relating to the reality of the child in treatment. The situation is bound to provoke questions. How does one manage the information? Should the child be told? If so, what is the therapist's position? If not, what does one do in the countertransference with information that is known but not communicated?

We each respond in our own way to these questions. My present concern is to raise the problem of *the unconscious repercussions of these situations on the therapist's work.*

In a very general way, I personally think that information considered by the therapist to be *important* should be communicated to the child. Too much information, however, to my mind, risks introducing an intrusive and persecuting element and may also bias the therapeutic work towards a form of pedagogic intervention resting on unconscious collusive complacency. However, the therapist must be able to manage adequately the compromise between "honesty towards the child" and protection of the therapeutic process. By contrast, the countertransference problems presented by the need not to communicate which is sometimes imposed by the parents is well known; it illustrates the unconscious countertransference pitfalls of such a situation. How, for example, is one to interpret dispassionately phallic–narcissistic manifestations—which can undoubtedly be part of the process—in the knowledge of a school failure of which the child is still unaware?

The fantasy world

Even more complex, however, is the interference of the therapist's fantasies that are activated by her encounter with the actual parents on the identificatory games with the child and the fantasized parents. We cannot meet the parents without their *personalities* awakening fantasies in us; without the link with the child arousing conscious and unconscious reactions; without the way in which we perceive their experience of the therapist's role; without all of that flooding us and risking distortion of our understanding not only of the child's *imago fantasies* and object relations, but also of the "*transference*", supposedly the projection of those fantasies, and finally of our *therapeutic role*.

Understanding imago fantasies

I am thinking here of what the child reveals of his fantasy world through what he says, how he plays, his drawings, his imagination. The understanding of unconscious (or preconscious) fantasy scenarios that the child reveals demands from the therapist a process of identification with the child. Over and above what might be called a "blind spot", the interference of the therapist's own unconscious organization in this identificatory process, the representation, conscious and unconscious, that the therapist builds up of the actual parents of the child may constitute a surcharge hampering the understanding of the child. I am thinking of the difficulty a therapist has in interpreting the threatening monsters that a little boy repetitively represented as paternal castrating images whereas, in reality, the therapist met a father effaced and crushed by a "phallic" woman, a father whom the therapist justly accused of playing an insufficiently solid role.

Things are more complex, more subtle, and more charged with resistances at the level of the transference too.

The transference

The transference is always difficult to shoulder. Living through "the medium of imago projections"—the protagonist of strange fantasy scenarios, taking on the role of personages alien to one's own identity—is a perilous exercise. It means not only assuming the *imago* that the child attributes to us, but also entering into

the *scenario* that the child replays in the transference relationship. When I say "enter into", I do not mean reacting, *but living to
the full* what is being unfolded there and of which one is an active
part. In child therapy, the stakes are all the higher because the
"as if" is fragile, the impact more direct, and the affects often
violent. The *understanding* of what is played out in the transference may find itself distorted.

But here, too, the therapist's fantasies aroused by an encounter with the parents foster her resistance to taking on some
roles, lead to an unawareness of the reality of what is happening,
or provoke countertransference behaviour that expresses unconscious attitudes towards the parents.

Here is one example among many:

A female therapist is discussing in a group supervision a
child whose sessions often end in very manic behaviour with
everything being thrown into disorder. She ponders over this,
complaining that her young patient disturbs her schedule:
she needs a great deal of time to put things straight after the
passage of the whirlwind. Only after some time do the group's
questions become more precise: the therapist, as a rule, has
a tendency to some stringency in relation to her own intolerance of disorder. She always suggests to her patients that
they tidy up before the end of the session. What happens with
this particular patient? "But," she says, "I don't ask him to
tidy up." Amazement. Why not? "Why not? Because it is a
reaction linked to separation." But still? "Why do you want
me to demand such a thing of him? He is already subjected
all day to a mother whose perpetual demands strike me as
unbearable!"

The function of the child therapist

The function of the child therapist is a very complex one. Its
exercise puts one in a conflictive fantasy position between identifications with the role of *parent* and of *child*. On the one hand,
the understanding of the child means immersion in an infantile

world, which obviously takes the therapist back to her own childhood; whereas, on the other hand, the role of therapist is, whether one wishes it or not, an adult, parental role which is constantly revived by the child's projections. Furthermore, the function of child therapist involves the most fundamental narcissistic and object cathexes, which are at the basis of the therapist's professional identity. In addition, the questioning of the *therapist's function* by the parents touches on a *vulnerable area* in the therapist, leading to drifts in her functioning.

Now, as we know, the therapist's interference in the parents' own cathexis of the child in the family dynamics is experienced by them as very conflictive. The complex and conflictive way in which they experience the therapist (rivalry, dependency, destructiveness) cannot but "pass into" the parent–therapist contacts, activating or exacerbating problem areas in the therapist's pursuit of her work.

This has, of course, been spelled out in the other explanations I have presented: one parameter can be isolated only artificially from those I have considered. Nevertheless, I am bringing two examples of parental interference in which the questioning of the therapeutic *function* predominates, but which could as well illustrate the other viewpoints already considered.

Charles—
Example of an "attack" on the therapy by the parents

Charles' parents are divorced and remain in conflict. The mother broke off a first therapy before sending Charles to her female therapist. The latter had, with the mother's consent, written to Charles' father to meet him. At the same time, the mother sent Charles to "another doctor" whose role is not clear. She wanted the therapist to get in contact with this doctor, which annoys the therapist.

The session: Charles talks about the letter that the therapist has sent to his father. The therapist points to the importance Charles is attaching to the meeting with his father, but Charles denies this in order to carry on about the famous doctor, enlarging upon how well he got on with him and insisting that the therapist meet him. The two of them [the doctor and the therapist] could help Charles so much; the one without the other is not possible.

The group listening to this sequence understands it as the child's appeal to the idealized reparative couple formed by his therapist and "the doctor", a couple whose permission he awaits to meet his father represented by the "doctor".

But the therapist, uneasy at Charles' insistence, explains to him that they are both there to talk about it all, but that her way of working is not to meet the doctor—thus missing an *interpretation* of the situation in the terms in which we understand it as observers protected from the input of the countertransference.

Analysis of the countertransference enabled us to work out how threatened the therapist felt in her therapeutic role, attacked by the intrusion of a third person "better than her"— that is, by the mother. Her interpretative capacities were disrupted, but here, too, her intervention is not harmless: it is her *function* as therapist that she is justifying, explaining, and defending . . .

Linda—
Personal example

Linda is an 11-year-old whose main symptoms are centred around inhibition. Her essentially neurotic structure allows an "interpretative" psychotherapy centred mainly on the conflictual nature of her epistemophilic drives in an oedipal context. But the parents put my back up when I meet them, by their restrictive, petty bourgeois conformity. I have the feeling that Linda's opening out is continually up against the weight of the family yoke, especially her mother's.

The session: Linda comes to her session and explains at great length that she would like to go with her friend to hear a pop singer. Then she embarks on a messy painting activity in a regression that she tends to adopt when an element at a higher oedipal level in the material she has brought makes her uncomfortable. I hear myself giving her the following interpretation: "It seems that you are uncomfortable showing me your wish to be grown up and go and listen to a singer as if you were afraid it would be unacceptable and I wouldn't love you any more . . . *like Mum!*" And Linda starts crying, "Oh, yes, Mum certainly wouldn't love me any more."

Thinking over why I slipped up, I wondered about my rush to drop the transference role and bring in the mother. I had met her two days before. More than ever, she had struck me by her intolerance towards elements that I myself saw as proof that *our* work was progressing. Indeed, she had totally collaborated with the therapy, a support that ensured an almost obsessively rigorous setting. She trusted me completely. But Linda, she said, was beginning to show reluctance: too much schoolwork . . . would she still have to come for a long time? Did she really want to? She did not know.

Only in the aftermath of working through Linda's session did I realize the perfidiousness of the mother's insinuations, the impact she had had on me, and the violence of my feelings towards her. The way I had broken the transference movement too hurriedly was clear evidence of my sensitivity towards the mother's *destructiveness* with regard to my therapeutic function: I was putting back on her the violence that had made me intervene without due regard for the wound I was inflicting on the child.

I believe now that I was defending myself against an involvement, although an unconscious one at the time, brought about by the mother's indirect criticisms: my therapeutic work, *my role as therapist* jeopardized the family equilibrium *and created anxiety and unhappiness in Linda for which I was responsible.* By putting back onto the mother the responsibility for Linda's anxiety, I was clearing myself from responsibility and at the same time failing in my therapeutic transference role . . . a bitter awareness, which did, however, have the merit of initiating, a long time ago, the kind of questioning that every child therapist must consider throughout her practice.

Conclusions

In this chapter, I have pointed out some of the essential tasks of the work of the child psychotherapist and of child psychotherapy and how these are assisted by the setting offered. I have tried to show through clinical vignettes how contact with and pressures from the parents can, in a variety of ways, affect the therapist's work with the child through differing countertransference reactions to the parents. Having defined the symbolizing and interpretative functions of the therapist, I show how these can both be significantly affected by the differing kinds of countertransference responses to the parents. The clinical vignettes include demonstrations of how these countertransferences can cause shifts in focus away from the internal world of the child in therapy or shifts away from the child's transference to external realities. I also show that breakdowns can occur in the symbolizing function of the therapist due to emotions resulting from the impingement of the parents and other intrusions into the setting, including untoward consequences on therapy of meeting the parents in reality.

CHAPTER SEVEN

Different uses of the countertransference with neurotic, borderline, and psychotic patients

Anne Alvarez

T he Laplanche and Pontalis dictionary of psychoanalysis defines countertransference as "The whole of the analyst's unconscious reactions to the individual analysand—especially to the analysand's own transference" (1973). Like Hinshelwood's *A Dictionary of Kleinian Thought* (1989), it comments on the controversy about how wide to make the definition—for example, whether to include the analyst's own private emotional contribution or whether to narrow the definition to only those feelings aroused or evoked in the analyst by the patient. I give my own definition a little later, and then go on to discuss the importance, for our clinical work, of considering, a particular question: namely, the *effect* of our countertransference responses on the patient. We receive signals, but we also transmit them. The patient may project into us, but we then project something back

An earlier version of this paper was published in *Contrapunto: Materiali di Lavoro dell'Associazone Fiorentina di Psicoterapia Psicoanalitica.* No. 13. Some of the clinical material appeared in my book, *Live Company,* but is discussed here with reference to the issue of the countertransference.

into him. How does he introject this? The countertransference, I suggest, may be unconscious, or conscious but not yet processed: either way, it needs, as Irma Brenman-Pick (1985) has pointed out, working through in rather the same manner as does the patient's transference. What is taking place is a duet, not a solo. I do not here go into changes in the theory of transference as a result of the work of Bion, but partly also as a result of the findings from infant observation and infant development research. Now, for example, a fascination with lighting fires might not necessarily be seen as expressing sexual or bodily fantasies, but at least partly as representing a need to make an impact, to bring a light to some imaginary figure's eyes—that is, to *interest* someone.

It is probably well known that there is now considerably more attention to happenings in the here-and-now and, for some analysts and therapists, much less comment on the past, although there is recognition that the past may be being lived out in the present. The attention to and study of these on-going interactions in the present have been stimulated in Britain by theoretical developments following from the work of object-relations theorists such as Klein, Fairbairn, and Bion. There have been parallel developments in North and South America and Continental Europe as well (Bion, 1962; Fairbairn, 1952; Klein, 1937; Racker, 1968; Spillius, 1983; Sullivan, 1953).

A word about the concept of projective identification, which has become for Kleinians an essential element for work in the countertransference. (I point out that in two of the examples below, those concerning Robbie and Harriet, it plays less of a part in the countertransference.) Klein's work suggests that it is not enough to look for missing aspects of the patient in his repressed and buried unconscious: these missing parts or feelings could sometimes lie much further afield, in someone else's feelings. This phenomenon, called "projective identification", includes situations in which, for example, some people you meet always make you feel intelligent and attractive, while others always make you feel that your slip is showing. Human beings, often quite unknowingly, can evoke very specific and often powerful feelings in other people, and we may do this repetitively in certain systematic ways in order to rid ourselves of unwanted or simply unacknowledged parts of our own personality, or because we genuinely believe a particular feeling or thought or talent could never be ours. A child may, indeed, have an elder brother who is more intelligent or more academic than she is, but if this fact of her family history has led her to believe that everyone is more intelligent and that she is stupid, she may not only see others as more intelligent (Freud's notion of projection), she may be doing something much more active and continuously impoverishing to her own personality than simply having a perception: she may really be allowing or even inviting others to do the thinking for her in situations where she could do it for herself (projective identification as described by Melanie Klein and developed by her followers: Bion, 1962; Klein, 1946; see also Freud, 1911c [1910]).

The therapist of such a girl may need to explore in herself, then, how it is that this patient, Laura, always makes her feel so protective and intelligent and wise. To discuss these observations with the patient and show her how these processes keep repeating themselves moment by moment in the sessions seems to be far more effective than simply resorting to elaborate detective-like reconstructions about the past causes of the patient's beliefs about herself. Links with the past are, of course, important, but they are no substitute for the study of the living interactions and of the often dangerous erosions of precious parts of the personality that may take place in these interactions (Joseph, 1989).

Laura was a mildly neurotic, depressed girl. With borderline or severely deprived or chronically depressed patients, the technical handling of the countertransference is very different. With them, the projective identification may arise out of a desperate need that the therapist hold feelings that the patient is genuinely incapable of holding for himself. At this point, if we are to consider the effect of our words and our emotionally toned comments on our patients, then we may need to think much about the tone, the grammar, and the *location* of our interpretations. It is important to assess our countertransference responses, but we also have to assess *what to do with them* and how to communicate them to the patient. This may involve considerations of something that I shall call perspective—the perspective or distance from which a patient can manage to tolerate an experience. It may be important, as Joseph (1989) has suggested, to allow the patient to explore the experience as it takes place *in us*, not in himself. This may depend on the developmental level at which the patient is functioning at any given moment.

A bit of history: Bion's use of projective identification as a normal process, his idea of the analytic object as container, and Rosenfeld's concept of the transference psychosis, led inevitably to the view that the psychoanalyst may not only play the part of the patient's objects and selves in the patient's mind, but in her own mind too (Bion, 1962; Rosenfeld, 1965). The patient may project depression, for example, so skilfully that he may not only feel his therapist is depressed, he may make the therapist *become* depressed.

Paula Heimann wrote a good deal about the transference and countertransference. In 1950 she criticized the analytic ideal of the "detached" and mildly benevolent analyst. Her thesis was that the analyst's emotional response to her patient within the analytic situation represented one of the most important tools for her work. Her countertransference, she claims, is an instrument of research into the patient's unconscious. She pointed out that both views originate with Freud (Heimann, 1950).

It may be important at this point to define the way in which I myself use the term countertransference, and also the ways in which I do not use it. I make use of the more narrow definition referred to by writers of the psychoanalytic dictionaries—that is, I refer only to those feelings aroused or evoked in the therapist by the patient (this is not to imply that the issue of the feelings' origins is always clear from the beginning!). However, the definition used herein is narrow in another sense; it would *not* include a perception of something going on in the patient which is not accompanied by a similar or related feeling in the therapist. For example, I do not think it is helpful to say, "my countertransference told me that the patient was depressed", unless for no apparent personal reason I suddenly felt depressed myself when with him. In fact, my eyes probably told me the patient was depressed. I would prefer to call this situation "empathic perception". That is, the statement "I could see that the patient was depressed" implies that the patient can convey his depression with body posture, facial expression, and tone of voice. Projective identification and countertransference, on the other hand, are important when the patient *does not know* he is depressed and may not even feel depressed and not appear depressed. Or when he spills it out very powerfully. Ordinary empathic perceptions are important when fairly ordinary communication processes within the patient's self and between himself and the therapist are working, but projective identification and countertransference are involved in the more extraordinary processes.

I wish now to say a little about Bion's concept of containment. His notion seems to be that if the mother is capable of something he calls reverie, the baby may project his frustrations, rages, and fears into her and get them back in a modified form (1962). The second half of the process—the getting back—he later called transformation (1965). He likened this to the activity of the artist, and also to the interpretive activity of the analyst. I would like to suggest that in fact the process can really be seen to be made up of four phases:

1. the receptive or containing stage when the material first makes its impact;
2. the transforming work that goes on inside the therapist;
3. the interpretive work, which may or may not involve returning the projections to the patient;
4. the *effect* of the interpretation on the patient—that is, how he hears it, for the effect may be different from the one the therapist intended.

I have already mentioned Laura, the depressed neurotic girl who was projecting her intelligence. In Laura's case, it was important for the therapist to show her, in the sense of give back to her, the projection of a part of herself that really belonged to her. This is possible even when the projection is of a bad unwanted part, as long as the patient has enough ego with which to look at, examine, and own the previously projected part. The situation is, I think, quite different with the three following borderline and psychotic cases. The first is a very brief but fairly classic example of a patient making use of what I think was a desperate type of projective identification both to evacuate and communicate terrible hopelessness and lifelong frustration. Here I will stress that the containing function, the first in the sequence of four stages, was most important. The therapist had to contain her countertransference, not give it back too prematurely.

Angie

Mrs G, a therapist in London, has been working with a very disturbed and despairing physically handicapped girl who has had a variety of surgical interventions and is permanently in a wheelchair. Angie, who is 13, has recently taken to giving her therapist "bad treatment" by wrapping Mrs G's legs in Sellotape and telling her she must stay there forever. It has been very moving to watch this girl emerge from her depression as she has begun to show, at first, her quite sadistic delight and pleasure in Mrs G's willingness to describe what it is like for her (Mrs G) to be in this plight. Mrs G is not just playing a game, of course. Faking the countertransference will not work. She finds the imagining and identifying with Angie's situation horrifying and quite agonizingly heartbreaking. But *at no point* does she at this stage remind Angie that this is really Angie's lifelong experience. The therapist understands and will, at a later stage, be able to interpret that Angie feels that *someone else ought to be having this terrible experience, not Angie.* The language of wishes and wants ("You wish you could have been born healthy") can weaken the child's ego; the understanding of emotional and moral imperatives may strengthen it. Angie will never walk, but her relief in watching someone be willing to undergo this experience, *even if only in fantasy*, is palpable. What began as a more cruel projection has changed to something on the way to being more playful, more communicative, and more symbolic. This situation, of course, is very different from the one with a more manic neurotic child who may need to face his depression. Angie probably knows more about depression and despair than we shall ever know. It is also different from work with the psychopathic hardened or sadistic child who relishes and enjoys making us suffer because it turns him on!

Robbie

In the 1960s, I became very concerned about the degree of mobility and activity called forth in me by a very withdrawn and passive autistic patient named Robbie. He was not the typical Kanner-type child who seems to be hiding in his shell (Tustin, 1981). He had no shell at all, and he seemed to be not hiding, but lost and dissolved. He had something in common with institutionalized children. I spent years feeling worried about the degree of alarm and urgency evoked in me by Robbie. Well-tried analytic technique has taught us that when the therapist overreacts to excessive projections, this can prevent the patient from getting in touch with his own feelings of urgency for himself. Yet under-reaction has perhaps been less well explored as a technical problem, with some exceptions (Carpy, 1989; Coltart, 1986; Symington, 1986; Tustin, 1981). I often found I had to call Robbie's name, move my head into his line of vision, and when he seemed at his utterly lowest ebb I felt extreme urgency and alarm and spoke to him in a manner that showed this. It was on one of these occasions one July, just before a long summer break, that he seemed to surface and greet me like a long-lost friend. It was also immediately after this that he had his breakdown, or rather break-out from his autism, and described a fantasy of where he and all his loved ones had been rescued from a dark well by a very long, long, long rope. I have come to think that the sense of cliff-edge urgency in the countertransference may, at certain moments with certain patients, have to do with carrying something for the patient that he is as yet *unable*—not unwilling—to carry for himself. (Rosenfeld, 1969, wrote of the analyst functioning as auxiliary ego for psychotic patients. Here, one is almost an auxiliary id, carrying the patient's sense of being alive.) The patient does not "wish" we would reclaim him—he is too ill and far-gone for that—he *needs* us to reclaim him.

Infant observation and infant research has shown that for his emotional and cognitive development, the baby needs to have experience of, and interaction with, a consistent human caretaker, an "animate object", or, in Trevarthen's phrase, "live company" (Spitz, 1946; Trevarthen, 1978). A major technical problem for the therapist is how to provide such experience to children who have difficulty in assimilating experience in general, and also a particular difficulty in assimilating the experience of a living human object. This seems to me to suggest a need for a notion that takes account of the perspective from which experience is had or viewed: notions such as the object's availability, its accessibility, graspability, proximity, and its perceptual followability. Bion's concept of containment suggests some of the conditions under which learning and introjection take place; but his concept, even at its most mental, tends to have metaphorical links with something concave, a lap-like mind, perhaps (see Grotstein, 1981). Sometimes, however, the container is soothing, at others it is seen as something much firmer. I have already suggested (Alvarez, 1992) that the maternal object needs also to be seen as *pulling the child, drawing the child, attracting the child, or interesting the child.* It may also need to seek the child and *be interested in the child.* I now want to stress another element, one that involves a metaphor that is more visual, and different in the tactile sense—a metaphor quite other than that of a lap or encircling arms. This arises from what is now known about the baby's need to have objects such as the mother's face, or her breast, presented—particularly in the early days of life—at *just the right distance* for the face to be seeable and the breast to be feedable from in a satisfactory way (Papousek & Papousek, 1976; Woolridge, 1986). The conditions under which babies are able to reach and grasp objects in three-dimensional space may also be of relevance to the question of the conditions under which an *idea* may begin to become graspable. Perhaps the developmental processes and stages involved in the functioning of the baby's eyes, hands, and even in the actual anatomy of its sucking have received less attention in the psychoanalytic models than they deserve.

The fact, for example, that an experience can only be assimilated when it is located in someone else *may have more to do with questions of perspective than with questions of projection.* Such locating may actually involve the *beginnings of an introjective process rather than a projective one.* The way in which a patient may or may not be able to follow his therapist's train of thought, or pursue one of his own, may be as analogous to the problem of the visual tracking of the trajectory of moving objects as to his response to the flow of milk in his throat (Bower, 1982).

Bion and Rosenfeld, both of whom worked extensively with psychotic patients, have hugely increased the understanding of the enormous power of the processes of projective identification in psychotic patients (Bion, 1965; Rosenfeld, 1965). It is important to remember, however, that the patients of Bion and Rosenfeld were adults, and that where these authors refer to the analyst carrying parts of the self that have been projected, the implication somehow is that it must have once belonged to the personality before projection. Work with very young psychotic children, however, often makes one suspect that this "projected" part may never have belonged to the personality in the first place, at least not in any solid way. It may need to grow, and this sense of being alive and human may need to be recalled, or, in the case of the illest children, called forth. This need in the patient for input from the therapist in order to be recalled to himself must always be carefully distinguished from the part of his personality which, as it were, can't be bothered to fight for life; the line between apathy consequent on despair and the apathy consequent on hostile indifference, complacent passivity, or masochistic wallowing is not an easy one to draw.

I will summarize and oversimplify the three examples so far described. In the first, that of the neurotic girl, Laura, it was important to use and transform the countertransference and to give a lost part of her personality back to her (returning a projective identification). In the second example, that of the handicapped girl, Angie, it was important at that stage to keep the despair and frustration in oneself (holding a desperately needed projective identification in oneself). In the third, that of the autistic boy, Robbie, it was important to be far more active, carrying a live feeling self and calling the patient back to himself and to live human contact by means of amplifications and reclamations (the patient seemed to be too ill to use projective identification, as he had given up).

There is a fourth, mixed case in which I think I needed to fulfil something like all three of the above at once, and this may have been a rare occasion when I managed it. It was always very difficult to get the balance right with this patient. This fourth example is of some work with a patient who was not flagrantly psychotic but nevertheless quite schizoid, withdrawn and out of touch with feeling. The example may illustrate the problem of keeping a balance between notions of a projective process that is excessive and one that is too weak and inadequate, perhaps because the experience has never yet been located anywhere. The thought may not so far have been thinkable.

Harriet

A very withdrawn adolescent patient of mine, a girl named Harriet, was involved, after some years in treatment, in a serious car accident. Although she was in a coma and close to death at one point, her life was saved by an operation that temporarily removed a piece of her skull—part of her forehead—so that pressure inside the brain could be relieved. She returned to therapy with this disfiguring hole in her head, and often expressed considerable anxiety and impatience for the operation to take place that would replace the missing piece of bone. After some months, the date was finally fixed when her local hospital would do the surgery. This meant that the bone had to be sent from the hospital in another city where the original operation had taken place. She (and I) had assumed that such a precious piece of a person would be sent by something like an ambulance or by courier. Or perhaps the first surgeon—who was both eminent and caring and had, after all, saved Harriet's life—would bring it himself! Harriet came in one day and said quite casually, and in her flattest of flat voices, that she had just heard it was being sent by post. There were postal difficulties in the area at the time, which we both knew about, and I felt a moment of absolute horror at this news. Harriet was, as I have said, not psychotic, and although at times she was very cut off from feelings out of a genuine depersonalization and difficulty in finding them, at other moments she was extremely skilled at projecting them. I knew from long experience with her that if I overreacted at such a moment—if, for example, I had revealed my own anxiety for the fate of her bone—she would simply ask me coldly and contemptuously what I was making such a fuss about. I also knew that if I tried too neutrally to insist that *she* felt horror or anxiety about her bone, she would deny it, feel nothing, and my attempt to put her in touch with herself would also fail. Betty Joseph (1989) has stressed the importance of not pushing parts of the patients self back at them prematurely or too crudely: she points out that the analyst may have to contain unassimilable parts for some while, and the patient may need to explore these in the analyst. I would add that, with the more withdrawn patients, in order for the process of containment, exploration, and eventual re-introjection of the lost part to begin at all, the patient first has to register that there actually is an emotional state worth exploring. I think I managed on that occasion to get the balance right. I pointed out to Harriet that she was telling me this fact without any feeling at all, yet she had previously been very worried about the arrival of the bone. I tried to show her how she seemed to be "posting" into me, with *truly terrible casualness*, a very precious part of herself, namely her feeling of anxiety about her bone. I did, I may say, put this interpretation to her with some feeling: I believe that if I had spoken too strongly, she would have closed up even more and projected the whole of the experience into me; on the other hand, if I had spoken too neutrally, or too slackly, or without sufficient seriousness, she would simply have experienced me and the feeling as too far away. As it was, she did really seem to hear the interpretation because she suddenly said, in for her a very spontaneous and relieved way, that she suddenly had realized how very worried she was. She rang the specialist later and the bone had been delivered safely, and the operation subsequently went well.

Perhaps it is the case that many people cannot be in touch with their own feelings until they have been in touch with *a* feeling. At that point, it hardly matters who has the feeling first. In fact, Harriet began to say with surprise that it was odd that someone else often had to feel things for her first, before she could feel them for herself. At such moments, I do not believe she was using other people as vehicles for ridding herself of unwanted parts of herself (only if I overreacted did it serve this projective function); rather, I think that she was using them as places for the tentative exploration of whether or not it was safe to have feelingful states of mind at all.

Rayner cites Matte-Blanco as suggesting that there are two distinct processes in the course of therapy. One is the lifting of repression and the undoing of defences; the other is an "unfolding or translating function". According to Rayner, this is "helping the patient to see new or deeper meanings in ideas that are not repressed but quite conscious". Rayner has pointed out that the patient usually quietly enjoys this sort of process as enhancing (Rayner, 1981 p. 410). Not all enhancements, of course, are pleasurable, but even unpleasant ones seem to be quite life-giving for cut-off patients. I believe Bion's concept of alpha function suggests that the thought may have to be thinkable long before the therapist should concern herself with luxurious questions about who is having it. During these mixed moments, the therapist may have to keep the part that belongs to him while trying to give the part that the patient needs to own back to him, and even add something more. I think I had to add the sense of alarm and urgency that Harriet could not feel or at that moment, even conceive of. Perhaps she had the faintest "preconception" of it (Bion, 1962). No wonder this work is difficult. I have given an example of a rare occasion when I got the balance right with a very fragile, tenuously in-touch girl. I do not wish to suggest that this was a particularly frequent occurrence!

Summary

I have tried to suggest that while the proper processing of the countertransference involves attention to the therapist's feelings and some idea of where in the patient the feelings may have originated, it also involves an anticipation of *the way in which the patient is going to be able to hear the interpretation.* This will depend on the level of the patient's emotional/cognitive development and the urgency of his needs. A wish is milder than an urgent developmental need. In the first example, that of the neurotic girl, Laura, it was possible to return her projections to her relatively easily. Her projections were not desperate, nor was her ego incapable of processing the re-introjection. In the second example, that of the handicapped girl, Angie, it was necessary to hold the feelings in the therapist (projective identification was operating, but as a desperate need for communication of something unthinkable (Bion, 1962). In the third case, that of the autistic boy, Robbie, he was too ill and lost to project, so the therapist had to go out to him and reclaim him and carry lifesaving and life-asserting functions. In the fourth case, the borderline schizoid girl, Harriet, the therapist had to perform all three functions. As therapists, we must pay attention not only to where our feelings of outrage, horror, despair, or sympathy came from, but also to where they are going and whether they should be returned, and how much of them, to the patient and in what form. This is much easier to write about than do!

CHAPTER EIGHT

Bisexual aspects of the countertransference in the therapy of psychotic children

Didier Houzel

To each level of organization of the mind corresponds an aspect of bisexuality. In my view, we can distinguish three such levels, corresponding to successive stages of individuation and construction of the child's inner world. The first relates to the frontier structures of the mind, which Esther Bick (1968) called psychic skin and Didier Anzieu (1986) was later to call the skin ego or psychic envelope. The second level is that of part-object relations, and the third corresponds to whole-object relations. At each of these levels of mental organization, maternal and paternal functions interact in a complementary manner. They are integrated with the corresponding structure, which as a result possesses bisexual features. Flaws in this integration may give rise to various types of psychopathological disorder; in therapy, we are continually faced with defective integration of bisexuality. Before describing the nature of the problem encountered with psychotic children, I first distinguish the respective characteristics of bisexuality at the three levels of organization I have defined: psychic envelope, part-object relations, and whole-object relations.

The constitution of the psychic envelope has its source in maternal care—in particular, the feeding relationship. Esther Bick wrote that "the optimal [containing] object is the nipple-in-the-mouth together with the holding and talking and familiar-smelling mother" (Bick, 1968).

Frances Tustin drew our attention to the profound splitting we find in autistic children between contrasting sensory qualities: wet and dry, smooth and coarse, soft and hard, hot and cold, and so forth, qualities that she relates to the bisexuality of the early maternal container, the nipple-and-breast (Tustin, 1981). Geneviève Haag has also emphasized bisexuality in the oral relation (Haag, 1983).

In my opinion, a critical aspect of the psychic envelope is its elasticity. It has to be extensible and flexible so as to adapt to and accommodate the ebb and flow of drive demands; yet at the same time it must be strong and able to offer some resistance to these demands without bursting or losing all shape. These features are necessary if it is to accomplish its containing function and serve as a basis for the construction of the child's identity and for the development of his sense of reality. I would locate the extensibility and flexibility of the psychic envelope on the maternal side, and strength and resistance on the paternal one. Adequate integration of both aspects gives the psychic envelope the required elasticity.

It is not without interest to note that Freud borrowed the concept of bisexuality from his friend Wilhem Fliess, who thought he had discovered a 23-day periodic cycle in men, the equivalent of the female 28-day cycle. In the infant's early relationship to his mother, rhythm is undoubtedly one of the fundamental expressions of psychic envelope bisexuality: piano, followed by forte, a maternal beat then a paternal one. I had begun therapy with an autistic boy when he was 4 years old; after four years of analysis with four sessions per week, he expressed the rhythmic aspect of the psychic envelope by singing in a very pleasant and true voice the Bach chorales he had heard played on the organ. He would contrast almost to the point of caricature the softness of the melody and the power of the great organ thundering out the chords. I interpreted this to him as a combination of the maternal and paternal aspects of the sessions, which he experienced as receptive and welcoming on the one hand, and confining but strong on the other.

Of Fliess's various hypotheses, Freud retained that of the psychic bisexuality of all human beings. He made considerable use of this concept, soon forgetting what he owed to his friend—the climax to their quarrel in 1904. Freud did however reject the link Fliess had suggested between bisexuality and bilaterality. Though it is clear today that Fliess's biological hypotheses are without foundation, it is tempting to see in his bisexuality-bilaterality link the premises of Geneviève Haag's description of body-image construction as made up of two halves, one of which represents the mother and the other the baby, unity being ensured thanks to the paternal elements (Haag, 1985).

Didier Anzieu makes the highly convincing remark that while Freud borrowed the concept of bisexuality from Fliess, he realized that it resulted from identification with both parental figures and had no biological foundation as such. Freud was going through a bisexual transference in his relationship to Fliess at the time when he borrowed the idea: "Freud could feel," writes Anzieu,

> that psychic bisexuality does not derive from biological bisexuality: the latter kind of explanation has to do with infantile theories about sexuality, i.e. a purely mental process—and therein lies the psychoanalytical explanation. Freud was beginning to realize that it was this bisexual identification which he was experiencing so intensely in his "transference" relationship to Fliess. [Anzieu, 1973; translated for this edition]

I agree with Anzieu that the psychic envelope finds itself grafted onto the analytical setting through transference to the setting (Anzieu, 1986). The more or less split-off parts of the bisexuality of the psychic envelope will be evidenced not as Bleger (1967) suggests in a static way (a deposit of conglomerated nuclei), but in a much more dynamic fashion as attacks on the setting, the meaning of which will be discovered only by working through the countertransference.

What I mean by "transference to the setting" is the dynamic aspect of the relationship between the child and various component elements of the therapeutic situation. I would identify three such elements: temporo-spatial, contractual, and mental.

The temporo-spatial element in the setting is made up of the frequency, regularity, length, and location of the therapy sessions. The psychotic child is particularly sensitive to these aspects. Any change is immediately noticed, any unusual trace in the therapy-room is immediately interpreted, every discontinuity in time revives violent fantasies of being torn away, excluded, falling—perhaps even disintegration, liquefaction, leaking away into nothingness, and so forth.

The contractual element in the setting involves the clear statement of the reasons for the joint presence of child and therapist in the same place. The psychotic child is seldom able to show much interest in this aspect of the setting, but he is very sensitive to the fact that there is agreement between his parents and the therapist on the aims and means of the therapy. James Gammill stresses that this aspect is present in all analyses with children, and he gives a thoughtful description of the traps into which a therapist may fall in her work with parents, as well as pointing out the different features of the parental transference onto the therapist and the latter's countertransference in her relationship to the parents (Gammill, 1989).

Recently, I had the difficult experience of a therapeutic mis-alliance with parents whose child had a severe symbiotic psychosis.

I was involved in the case as consultant, not as the actual therapist. The boy was making good progress with the therapy: language, play, and social skills were all improving. In spite of this, the parents were continually raising doubts about the need for therapy, letting their son miss sessions, and reducing their frequency. At the outset, he had three sessions per week, then it became necessary to reduce them to two when he began to attend day-hospital on a part-time basis. When his attendance at the day-hospital increased, the parents decided unilaterally to reduce the frequency of the therapy still further, this time to just one session per week— which, to my mind, was manifestly insufficient. I felt it neces- sary to make a show of authority, making my dissent clear and protesting against this breach of the therapeutic contract. The result was that the parents broke off all contact with me. During the telephone conversation in which the mother announced her decision not to meet with me any more, she told me of another break that had occurred some seven years previously, this time with the hospital paediatrician who had treated their first child, a 6-month-old baby suffering from a severe metabolic condition. The paediatrician wanted the baby transferred to Paris where there was a more appropriate specialized unit. The parents refused. "We were right to say no," said the mother, "because the baby died the following night." Were they not, in fact, extremely guilty at not having authorized the transfer? Perhaps they were thinking that the baby might not have died had he been admitted to the Parisian unit. Were they projecting into me this terrible guilt, which had created such a deep rift between them that to function as a couple and as parents was so severely jeopardized that their second child had developed a psychosis? I had been provoked by the violence of their projections into a kind of acting out that I ought to have avoided—though perhaps it was just not possible to avoid it.

Betty Joseph (1989) has shown that some countertransference actings out cannot be avoided and that our task is to analyse them afterwards in order to understand them fully. This is exactly what I tried to do in the present case. The deep sense of guilt I felt led me to think that the parents had projected into me their own strong feelings of guilt, which were impossible to work through—with the result that a deep rift was created as regards their parental roles: the mother was over-indulgent and over-protective towards her son, while the father showed excessive control and strictness almost to the point of violence. The question then became how to think through, in collaboration with the therapist and the day-hospital staff, the projections and splittings that were deposited in us, and in this way prevent them being an obstacle to the therapy and to the weaving together by the child of a bisexual psychic envelope.

Lydia

I was faced with a different aspect of the difficulties inherent in the therapeutic alliance with a family in another case. This was a little girl who suffered from a severe autistic syndrome coupled with epilepsy which was very difficult to stabilize.

Lydia was 3 years old when I began therapy with her on a three-session-per-week basis. Separating her from her mother could only be achieved gradually, but this was managed after about two months of therapy. Then came the Christmas holiday, the first interruption in the sessions. After the holiday, Lydia would no longer come into the room on her own; she clung to her mother and cried if I tried to separate them. I had to let the mother come back into the sessions.

After two months of mother–daughter sessions, I decided, with the mother's consent, to attempt another very gradual separation. I suggested that the mother leave ten minutes before the end of the session and that we gradually increase the time Lydia would be spending alone with me. This was done. From time to time Lydia would accept the separation, but at other moments she would cling to the door-handle, sobbing noisily. One day the mother brought Lydia along to her session accompanied by her own mother, Lydia's maternal grandmother. That day, Lydia wailed even more loudly, and both mother and grandmother on the other side of the door could quite clearly hear her crying. I felt like a mother disqualified as to her role, and judged severely by the grandmother behind the door. In a subsequent meeting with the parents—and without mentioning my countertransference experience—I learned from them that this grandmother, who acted as Lydia's childminder, would consent to all her whims and make disqualifying remarks concerning the parents, who were very sensitive to these. After this episode, during which I was able to contain the projections of Lydia's family and work through them in my countertransference, Lydia was able to stay alone with me for the entire session, and I no longer had to face any outbursts of noisy crying. Her parents needed to project into me their experience of being disqualified with respect to their role as parental containers.

The third element in the setting is the mental or psychic aspect. The mental setting is constituted by the analyst's listening and attentiveness and is, of course, the essential feature of the setting—the temporo-spatial and contractual elements are there simply as containers for it. This time it is the countertransference initiated by the child himself that guides us towards discovering and working through the defects in the psychic envelope as they are expressed in the transference to the setting. Recently, a psychotherapist reported a psychotic child's sessions that illustrate transference to the setting of a dehiscent psychic envelope.

Miguel

Some weeks previously Miguel had said to his therapist: "We won't be able to go on with the sessions if you don't talk to Mummy." Miguel had been taken into foster care under a care-and-protection order after suffering serious neglect. He sees his mother regularly, and she plans to take him back on a full-time basis. The psychotherapist had already met the mother, but the proposal to offer Miguel psychotherapy had been made to the foster-parents before that meeting. No doubt Miguel was asking the therapist to meet his mother because of the imminence of the latter's plan to take him back; but on a deeper level he could feel that something important was going on in his therapy, something that he would not be able to contain if he remained unsure of the solidity of the alliance between the therapist and his mother. I was able to help the therapist to understand the importance of Miguel's request; she could then decide to meet the mother at an earlier date than she had initially planned and speak to Miguel about it. She did this in the following session, telling Miguel that she had made an appointment with his mother and they would be meeting soon.

Miguel, who had been mute in his sessions since making his request, began once more to talk and also to draw. He drew a house; this, to my way of thinking, illustrates the integration of the bisexual aspects of his psychic envelope, enabling him to construct a solid and receptive container into which he could project the contents of his mind. Indeed, he went on to do this immediately, setting up a play sequence with dolls reminiscent of a primal-scene fantasy.

In order to use those normal projective mechanisms that enable psychic birth to take place, there has to be a space into which projections can be made. Esther Bick stressed this point in her description of the psychic skin. Later, Meltzer returned to the question, showing how the autistic child is unable to use these mechanisms because there is no psychic skin to delimit an internal space for the object and an internal space for the self (Meltzer et al., 1975). As soon as this frontier structure is constituted, part-object relations become possible. The child can project parts of the self into the object and introject his objects into an internal mental space.

The classic distinction between part-object and whole-object is based, on the one hand, on the underlying pre-genital or genital cathexis and, on the other, on cathexis of a part or whole of the object's body. While this remains valid, a third factor should also be taken into account: a part-object possesses physical and mental characteristics, but no internal organization—it has no specific structure. On the other hand, the whole object does have internal organization, with internal mental spaces and temporal structure and history—in other words, it is a person. Part-object relations are characterized by the search for certain qualities of the object that are not only physical or sensory but also mental. All of these qualities are categorized according to bisexual criteria: on the feminine/maternal side we find such aspects as receptivity, malleability, physical and emotional warmth, comfort, devotion, and so forth; on the masculine/paternal side we find strength, solidity, reliability, orientation, and so on. The combination of both types is necessary for constructing a balanced inner world enabling progress to the following stage, that of whole-object relations—the gateway through which the child enters the world of human communication, the oedipal adventure and object love.

I must emphasize that reciprocal mediation between maternal and paternal part-objects is vital. The maternal part-object would be overwhelming, engulfing, annihilating if it were not combined with a paternal part-object to balance and limit its operation. A sculpture by Camille Claudel springs to mind, "The Wave", where a tiny figure is about to be engulfed by an enormous wave towering above it. On the other hand, the paternal part-object would be threatening, aggressive, persecutory, and amputating if it were not tempered by the maternal part-object. Each has to usher in the other and act as mediator within an appropriate bisexual equilibrium. If mediation is unsuccessful, various forms of primitive anxiety may ensue. One possible outcome among those most often encountered is the fantasy that the paternal part-object has been sequestrated.

Jacques Lacan borrowed the legal term foreclosure to describe the complete absence of integration of the paternal function in the child's psychic world; as a result, the child is wholly dependent on the mother in an alienated psychotic relationship (Lacan, 1966). Though I am referring to the same kind of psychopathological situation, I prefer to think of it from a dynamic and interactive point of view. My argument is that if the paternal function cannot be brought into play, it is not because of foreclosure of the paternal object (Lacan's name-of-the-father) but because the paternal object is sequestrated and therefore inaccessible. A positive therapeutic outcome is possible as long as the sequestration fantasy can be analysed and worked through in the transference and countertransference. The typical fantasy scenario shows a maternal part-object holding the paternal counterpart prisoner, like Calypso keeping Odysseus in captivity.

Bernard

Bernard is a 6-year-old psychotic boy who began analysis at age 4½, with three sessions per week. The session I am about to report took place a little over a year into the therapy. His therapist is a woman, Mrs B. Just before he has his session, I occupy the same therapy-room with another boy, Alain. On this occasion, Bernard is waiting for his therapist on the other side of a small barrier blocking off a staircase. He shouts out, "Alain! Alain!" to the other boy, whom he can see coming out of his therapy session. Then he rushes into the room before his therapist has time to prepare it. She makes him leave. He takes a long drink from a Coca-Cola bottle he has brought with him. The session begins.

The therapist talks of his thirst when he comes to see her, and his fear that his greediness might empty her if he doesn't first of all fill himself up by taking a drink. She adds that he is very inquisitive about Mrs B's house when Alain is in it. Bernard replies, "Alain, I'm going to see Alain!" and makes as though to leave the room to be with the other little boy. He puts some water into a cup and some more into the feeding-bottle, then takes a big drink. "You're very thirsty," says the therapist, "when we meet again after three days' absence [this is the first session of the week and comes after a three-day break]. Maybe you're afraid there won't be enough to drink, or that Alain has taken it all."

Bernard pours the water out of the cup onto the floor, picks up the feeding-bottle, and drinks from it in a corner of the room near the desk. Then he places a chair near the cupboard containing the individual boxes in which children in therapy put away their playthings; he climbs up onto the chair and tries to get hold of the keys he knows are on top of the cupboard. He can't reach them. He pulls up an armchair, tries to climb up onto it, still with the idea of reaching the top of the cupboard. The therapist holds him back so that he won't fall, and explains that she can't allow him to take the keys. He tries to grab the therapist's spectacles. She has the impression that Bernard is acting out a fantasy about breaking-in and that he's terrified by it. He yells out, "Let me go!" but still clings to her. She points out that he seems to be feeling imprisoned by her. He drinks more water from the feeding-bottle, then pours the rest out onto the floor. Stamping his feet in the puddle, he marches all round his therapist, leaving damp footprints, and says, "Lost! I want to go home!" The therapist thinks of little Tom Thumb, of whom Bernard had spoken in previous sessions. He wants to go back to his mother. He says, "Mummy gone!" The therapist stops him leaving the room and says that when he poured water on the floor maybe he felt all jumbled-up with Mummy-B, as if he were imprisoned inside her. He again goes round the room, this time leaving wet handmarks on the floor. "You're leaving your traces," says the therapist, "like little Tom Thumb, so you can find your way back." She's thinking of the last session of the week, which has been cancelled, and says this to him. He picks up a pencil and tries to force it into an electric socket. The therapist intervenes. He then tries to put it into a small hole in the wall. She again stops him, and speaks of his desire to penetrate inside her to find out what will be happening on Saturday (the day of the cancelled session). He takes a black pencil and begins writing large B's on the wall. The therapist lets him do this, saying, "You want to write big Bernards inside Mummy-B and take up all the space; you want to keep me just for yourself." He climbs up on to the desk, holds out his arms to the therapist, and says, "Help." She replies, "You want me to help you like a Daddy-B, so that you won't feel all fallen-down on Saturday." By this time he has slipped down from the desk; he draws back the curtains, goes towards the radiator, and says, "Hotter radiator." He glances outside, a wistful look on his face. He says, "The captain's gone . . . constipated." He walks all round the room, comes back to the desk, touches it, and says, "I'm breathing." The therapist interprets: "You're feeling sad, you'd like to find a good Mummy-B to warm you up and a Daddy-B to stop you from falling." He searches for the pencil-sharpener and begins to sharpen some pencils. He becomes quiet and calm. "Make sharp pencils that work fine," he says. He hides under the desk and goes on sharpening his pencils, then comes out again and asks the therapist to help him: "Make bigger! More! More!", he exclaims.

The therapist talks about big Daddy-pencils which help him to write his name. He licks at his hands which are stained by the pencil-leads, and pretends to swallow his coloured fingertips.

This session demonstrates the child's urgent need to intrude into the fantasy spaces of the mother/therapist's body not only to chase rivals away and obtain sole possession, but also to reach the paternal object which is felt to be sequestrated inside the maternal object. Donald Meltzer (1966) describes a fantasy of intrusive identification with these spaces of the mother's body; associated to anal masturbation, its function is to deny separation from the object by substituting a fantasy of omnipotent possession. I would suggest that the kind of identification Meltzer describes aims not only to possess the maternal object which can then be controlled from the inside, but also to make contact with the paternal object sequestrated within the maternal object. Thus understood, new light is thrown on the claustrophobic anxieties that Meltzer describes as linked to fantasies of intrusive identification with the anal space of the mother's body: these anxieties are related at least in part to identification with the sequestrated paternal object. It is in this sense that I understand Bernard's enigmatic "the captain's gone . . . constipated". The paternal object is represented initially by the out-of-reach keys, then by the pencils Bernard can reach and, indeed, make use of once his therapist gives her interpretation in terms of the paternal transference. Access to the paternal object enables mediation to operate in relation to the maternal object—that is, it becomes possible to approach it without danger, to come back out again and possess the instrument, which opens the way to symbolization, represented here by the big Daddy-pencils which Bernard can use for writing.

And this is the point at which the world of whole-object relations becomes accessible. This is where I shall conclude, for we are now entering the world of neuroses, where bisexuality takes on the shape of infantile sexual theories and primal-scene fantasies which, as we know, are at the heart of neurotic disturbances. Therapy with psychotic children helps us discover the necessary preconditions for the advent of the oedipal conflict. We learn also how important the countertransference messages are in detecting flaws in psychic bisexuality at a primitive level, and how vital it is to think through our countertransference thoroughly enough in order to activate (or reactivate) the processes that guarantee its integration.

CHAPTER NINE

Transference and countertransference issues in the in-patient psychotherapy of traumatized children and adolescents

John Tsiantis

Introduction

I n this chapter, the phenomena of transference and countertransference observed during the application of psychoanalytic psychotherapy as part of the in-patient care of traumatized adolescents are presented and discussed.

My views represent an attempt to summarize some theoretical issues presented in the literature and to tender my observations made during the in-patient treatment of such children and adolescents (aged 8 to 15 years) in the in-patient unit of the Department of Psychological Paediatrics of the "Aghia Sophia" Children's Hospital, Athens.

A modified version of this paper was presented at the Fourth International Congress, "Trauma in Adolescence", of the International Society for Adolescent Psychiatry, Athens, July 1995.

I am thankful to the staff of the in-patient unit of the Department of Psychological Paediatrics and in particular to Mrs Bithari, psychotherapist of the unit, for sharing with me the clinical material presented in this chapter.

Laplanche and Pontalis, in *The Language of Psychoanalysis*, give the following definition of psychic trauma: "An event in the subject's life defined by its intensity, by the subject's incapacity to respond adequately to it, and by the upheaval and long-lasting effects that it brings about in the psychical organisation" (1973, p. 465).

Laplanche and Pontalis contend that, in his early writings, Freud tended to put the concept of trauma in an economic—that is, quantitative—perspective. Freud later said (1916–17): "We apply it [the term trauma] to an experience which within a short period of time presents the mind with an increase of stimulus too powerful to be dealt with or worked off in the normal way, and this must result in permanent disturbance of the manner in which energy operates." To put it another way, the psychological trauma is any psychological event that suddenly floods the ego, preventing it from securing a minimal sense of safety, and hindering the intact and integrated functioning of the ego. As a result, the ego is overwhelmed with anxiety, while the sense of complete helplessness that is also present contributes to bringing about an almost inevitable change in the psychological organization. In other words, the trauma leads to disturbance of the functions of the ego in that it narrows the range of techniques and patterns of behaviour available for dealing with objects and the environment (Furst, 1986). The following points regarding psychological trauma should also be noted as of great importance in understanding and coping with psychopathological phenomena. It is very often the case that a truly traumatic experience is invested with the fantasies *already existing* in the mind of the child or adolescent, and so an experience of physical violence or punishment, or a surgical operation, can be experienced as castration, as punishment, or as masochistic gratification. Here, the fantasies already present will appear to have been validated and reinforced, and the younger the child is, the greater will be the confusion between fantasy and reality. As noted by Kris (1978), the trauma also tends to become bound up with the events *subsequent* to it. He also observes that children and adolescents tend to confuse trauma and punishment. Psychologically traumatized children and adolescents are often convinced that they are "very bad", and they tend to be strongly inclined towards self-censure with resulting guilt and low self-esteem. They very often identify with the aggressor, and also with the guilt and defence mechanisms of the parents. As a result, adolescents who have been physically or sexually abused tend to repeat the same acts with other persons, while at the same time having shared fantasies and defences with the parents or others who abused them, with whom they enter into a conspiracy of silence. Another consequence of traumatic experience is regression to earlier developmental levels of organization. This regression can be in the services of development or can lead to libidinal and genetic fixation points. Nor should we forget that sensitivity to the trauma and the consequences of the trauma will vary in accordance with the stages of development that have already taken place. Furst also argues, in connection with the relationship between trauma and development, that the developmental tasks of each subsequent period will be affected. In the case of adolescence, he contends that while trauma will interfere with the developmental tasks of adolescence in a general way, the following specific vulnerabilities should also be noted:

1. Adolescents show marked oscillations between progressive and regressive movements. The regressive swings are often non-defensive, and in the service of development. The defensive regression induced by trauma, added to (the normal) regressive developmental swings, will tend to overwhelm the progressive forces and make the regression permanent.

2. As Blos (1962) has pointed out, adolescence is characterized by sensitivity to special circumstances such as object loss, passive dependency, loss of control and diminished self-esteem. These are often based on past trauma.

3. The heightened mobility of adolescence favours acting out. The traumatized adolescent will therefore tend to act out, instead of remembering and gradually mastering trauma by reworking it intrapsychically. In addition, the acting out may become permanently integrated into his personality organisation. [Furst, 1986, pp. 37–38]

I describe below some phenomena that seem to be observed in almost every in-patient unit for disturbed children and adolescents. Moreover, in such units these phenomena are too intense and difficult to cope with, placing great pressure on the staff and affecting their therapeutic interventions particularly when they try to apply individual psychoanalytic psychotherapy to psychologically traumatized and severely deprived children and adolescents. The predominant phenomena are those of impulsiveness, intense competitiveness, acting out, large-scale regression, and the mechanisms of denial, splitting, and projective identification. In conjunction with the application of individual psychoanalytical psychotherapy in in-patient units, those phenomena provide fertile ground for the development of complex phenomena of transference and countertransference. They also set up special types of pressure and difficulty within the unit itself. These factors need to be taken into consideration, understood, and dealt with in order to safeguard as far as possible the therapeutic approach to psychologically traumatized children and adolescents. Even though this volume is concerned primarily with countertransference issues, I think that the phenomena of transference and countertransference are so much interwoven that it is logical to discuss issues related to transference also.

Transference and countertransference and in-patient psychotherapy

Transference

In connection with transference, one of the basic differences between in-patient individual psychotherapy and out-patient individual psychotherapy is that, in in-patient treatment, the phenomena of transference are directed not only towards the therapist, but also towards the other members of staff and the institution itself.

As a functional space, the hospital is never neutral enough for individual psychotherapy; to some extent, it is possible to achieve the desired degree of neutrality in the private consulting-room. Extreme complexity is caused by the multiple reactions of transference and countertransference that develop among the children, the adolescents, the parents, the therapists, the nurses, and the other staff. This considerably complicates the situation, since it has to be discussed and comprehended by the staff as well as by the children or adolescents and by their parents.

Another important component in the application of individual psychotherapy to an in-patient setting is that the objects of transference (i.e. the staff members) are directly known to the therapist, who has a working relationship with them (Muir, 1987). In her contacts and work with the staff, the therapist will be informed about events in the everyday life of the unit which involve the child or adolescent. When working in an out-patient setting, the therapist does not usually possess first-hand knowledge of important events in the adolescent's life. The therapist, of course, finds out about such events through the communications from the parents, but even this knowledge will usually come in the form of reports on the work done with the parents or another worker. In other words, in this case, information reaches her as it is seen by the parents, while in the case of the in-patient unit it comes direct from the other staff of the unit. In both cases, of course, the material may have been affected by feelings of countertransference: those of the worker who sees the parents, or those of the other staff members. Theoretically, the material might be more distorted in the former case. Of course, the therapist is able to make direct observations. The therapist may use some or all of this additional material. To sum up, the setting of the therapy as part of in-patient treatment complicates the phenomena of transference and countertransference and, consequently, makes the work of the therapist more difficult.

Care for the traumatized adolescent outside the sphere of psychotherapy is provided by the nursing staff in separate areas, and the relationship between the nurses and the adolescents is a different one. Therapists tend to be more neutral, while the relationship between the nursing staff and the adolescents is more direct, sometimes revolving around themes such as the issuing of permission and prohibitions and the setting of boundaries. As expected, adolescents, especially traumatized adolescents, react in different ways, displaying different aspects of themselves to the two parties (therapist and nurses) and tending to see the therapist as "good" and the nurse as "bad". This can result in the child or adolescent being more inhibited with the therapist, reserving all his aggression to be vented on the more vulnerable nurse. The consequence of this is the emergence of a degree of splitting that would appear to be inherent in the character of the therapeutic structure. In the field of countertransference, too, the therapist tends to develop a corresponding positive and maternal countertransference towards the child or adolescent, thus reinforcing the child or adolescent in projecting his negative emotions onto the nurse, making her countertransference more intensely negative, and strengthening the splitting still further. There is, in other words, a tendency for the therapist to be idealized as "all good" and the nurse as "all bad". Here, of course, it is the nurse who—coming into everyday contact with the adolescent—has constantly to absorb the adolescent's aggression. This will tire her and cause her to feel at a disadvantage compared to the therapist, who often is a doctor, is in a position to produce interpretations, and can enjoy the luxury of being with the child or adolescent under the special conditions of therapy. As a result, the nurse may ask the therapist to intervene on a practical level in coping with the practical problems involved in the adolescent's behaviour. This state of affairs is particularly common when there is a lack of good communication and cooperation between the therapist and the nurse. The adolescent may become aware of this and play on the conflict, adding to the splitting. As a consequence, the therapist may actually be forced to intervene, thus losing her neutrality towards the child or adolescent. This will make the therapeutic relationship more difficult and will affect the therapeutic effectiveness of the milieu since the therapist–nurse relationship has been contaminated. If, however, the level of communication between the therapist and the remaining staff of the unit is satisfactory, then it will be possible to work through the complex phenomena of countertransference between the adolescent and the therapist and the remaining staff members. This can be seen in the following case.

An adolescent boy, N

N is an adolescent aged 13 years who has been receiving psychoanalytic psychotherapy twice a week for the last eight months on account of a severe obsessive-compulsive symptomatology with pre-psychotic elements accompanied by disorder of his sexual identity.

N's father abandoned the family when N was 3½ years old because of the father's very bad relationship with his wife, who displays a psychotic structure. The loss of N's father in this sensitive period of his life—as well as what preceded and followed this loss and the extremely bad relationship between his parents—undoubtedly caused a series of traumatic experiences. Four years ago, the father remarried and has a daughter by that marriage, which N only discovered while in treatment. N's mother refused to accept this fact and assigned to N the role of bringing the father back or taking revenge on him.

At the beginning of his first period of in-patient treatment, N began psychoanalytic psychotherapy twice a week. During the second period of in-patient treatment, during which communication with the parents had broken off, he began to display in therapy a transferential movement of oedipal content whose objects were the (female) therapist and a (male) nurse, representing the therapeutic setting. This movement was stimulated by a real event. Shortly before the wedding of another colleague, the therapist and the nurse had a meeting to discuss preparations for the wedding and to record a music cassette. The door of the office was shut and N attempted to eavesdrop on their conversation. At the next session, N talked about this meeting and, in an attempt to bring about splitting, spoke disparagingly to the male nurse (with whom he had a good relationship). With the help of the therapist, N was able, first of all, to connect his feelings about the nurse with the event that had stimulated them and with his feelings about the (female) therapist. He was also able to connect those feelings with the "dirty thoughts" and "microbes" that filled his obsessions. This development made it possible to use the psychotherapeutic sessions to explore issues revolving around N's sexuality and his guilt over his father's departure from the family at a time in N's development when he was attempting to resolve his oedipal conflict. His father's departure and the loss experienced by N had caused him a psychological trauma; moreover, this trauma was exacerbated by the way in which his mother had been exploiting him in making him responsible for bringing his father back. This highly intelligent adolescent had displayed emotional flatness and an absence of psychological thinking (which he himself described as "prohibitive"). We believe that what was initially responsible for reactivating fantasy capacities and further non-traumatic repetition was the excellent relationship between N and both his therapist and his nurse and the equally good relationship between the therapist and the nurse. Reactivation of fantasy capacities in connection with the earlier psychological trauma also allowed the therapist to discuss the psychological trauma related to the oedipal conflict.

On the other hand, splitting may be in the reverse direction: that is, the therapist's neutrality may be interpreted as a lack of interest, especially by deprived or traumatized children or adolescents, who form the great majority of those in in-patient treatment. The result will then be that the child or adolescent regresses still further in the relationship with the nurse, who will become "good" by comparison with the "bad" therapist (a shift further strengthened when the nurse "gives" to the child continuously and without limitation). This factor may be particularly acute in units where there is considerable rivalry between the therapists and the nursing staff, resulting often in the gratification by the nursing staff of the needs of traumatized and deprived children or adolescents. This splitting—that is, the "good nurse" and the "bad therapist"—may be reinforced by the behaviour of the adolescents themselves. Needless to say, there has to be good cooperation between therapists and nurses if splitting is to be overcome. Furthermore, the adolescent must see that the therapists and the nurses work together, and must experience this cooperation. This can take the form, in practice, of the community meetings, at which all the staff and the children or adolescents come together two to three times a week.

The staff will usually need a great deal of help before they can withstand the stress of being in effective contact with the patients. In most cases, this will be possible if there are good relationships and attachments among them, and if they are able to work with an outside consultant who will facilitate their gaining a better understanding of their patients and the problems that there may be in relations between them (James, 1987;

Menzies Lyth, 1985). The objective of systematic cooperation among the members of the team is to provide satisfactory solutions to administrative issues and to handle cases in which splitting between the therapists and the nursing staff has occurred. It is very difficult to combine and blend psychotherapeutic intervention with case management in the correct manner, although we should never forget that case-management decisions can be of great therapeutic value. This is equivalent to the provision of adequate maternal care (Winnicott, 1965). The psychotherapist's interaction with the other staff members (director, social workers, nursing staff, teachers) is quite complex and affords scope for the development of countertransference reactions that may have an adverse effect on the outcome of psychotherapy and on the therapeutic quality of the setting. In the particular case of psychologically traumatized children or adolescents, the delicate relationship and balance between individual therapy and the unit setting is subjected to greater pressure and may prove to be fertile ground for the development of intense countertransference reactions, with an impact on therapy. Adolescents tend to react to internal tensions such as anger, anxiety, or worry by acting on the environment rather than by changing themselves. This phenomenon is, of course, even more marked in traumatized adolescents, because of the difficulties and deficiencies they have in exercising internal control. Furthermore, the trauma may have the effect of eliciting perverse responses to normal needs: for example, an adolescent in great need of affection may behave so aggressively or misleadingly as to provoke rejection or exploitation. This confirms his worst fantasies of worthlessness and of the hostile nature of external reality. Perverse and aggressive behaviour may become a habit, and the adolescent is isolated from his affectionate feelings. Because of their deficiencies in internal control, such patients require a more highly structured holding environment. Adolescents of this kind react to internal tension by taking action in the form of becoming aggressive, competitive, and destructive. If this is restrained, the patient may begin to defend himself with the mechanism of projective identification. In such circumstances, the staff may be seen as aggressive, sadistic mothers and actually function in such a way; alternatively, they may absorb, metabolize, restrain, and detoxify the tension (Langs,

1979). This allows the adolescent to internalize his ability to regulate the tension rather than being flooded by it. Here, again, of course, we see the quality of the adequately good mother with her ability for reverie and containment (Bion, 1962). According to Bion it is important that the mother take in the baby's communications, ponder over them, and respond in a meaningful way. If the staff of the unit is ultimately capable of perceiving the ways in which the behaviour of the patients is evoking feelings in them, and if the staff are prepared to tolerate the tension and use their feelings to comprehend the patients, then they will avoid getting trapped in a countertransference role and becoming either the projected failed parent or the failed idealized parent. They will then function as the adequately good mother and will allow the psychotherapist the space he needs to explore, with the patient, the sources of his expectations and fears—that is, why parental figures become inadequate, rejecting, and traumatic. It needs to be recognized that the task of the therapist is a very difficult one. She has a dual role:

- She must be able to develop empathy with the patient and form a therapeutic relationship with the patient against the background of the therapeutic structure.
- At the same time, she is a member of a team, with a specific relationship to all the members of the team as individuals and as a team.

At the same time, it has to be remembered that the nursing staff are the cornerstone of the entire in-patient unit, and that without them no care can be provided. Let me add that in the case of units for difficult patients—for example, one for psychologically traumatized adolescents—the level of toleration of the unit as a whole seems to be identical to the stamina of the nursing staff.

One of the technical problems that requires discussion is that of interpreting transference. The question is how far interpretation relates only to the person of the therapist or is diffused through the institution and the in-patient unit. In some cases—especially those of traumatized children or adolescents, when the transference is aggressive or dependent—the therapist by her interpretative work may sometimes maintain the diffusion of the negative transference into other parts of the hospital or unit, thus reinforcing splitting. This would appear to be a defensive mode of interpretation on the part of the therapist, which enables the therapist to protect herself from being in contact with unwanted countertransference feelings. It is obvious that, in this situation, the therapeutic effectiveness of the setting will be affected.

Countertransference

We know that one significant aspect of in-patient therapy is the adolescent's effort to re-create, in the setting of the unit, real or fantasy components of the life he experienced before admission. These include the pathological relationships that have contributed to creating the patient's problem. In some cases of the in-patient treatment of psychologically traumatized children or adolescents—who, inter alia, tend to act out much of the time and to express their aggressiveness, and many of their transactions with the staff are control battles involving the setting and resetting of limits, a matter related to earlier experiences of severe deprivation and traumas—the staff can experience the stimulation of their unresolved feelings about aggressiveness and the setting of limits. The staff who are on the receiving end of projective identifications may react en masse, or provoke conflict between themselves, thus interfering with the therapeutic effectiveness of the setting.

Let me give an example.

At one point in the life of an in-patient treatment unit for children and adolescents, the patients included two or three rather aggressive and destructive adolescents. Their behaviour seems to have affected the other adolescents in the unit, almost all of whom became extremely demanding in an aggressive manner. Almost all the adolescents and children were provocative much of the time, constantly trying to break the limits and rules of the unit. Since the staff seem to have been more than usually afraid of the violence of the adolescents—and also of the impulse to counter-violence in them-selves, which of course was hardly a comfortable feeling for them—the result was the development of a regressive defence system in which the staff struggled to appease and placate the adolescents by shifting the problem elsewhere. They be-gan to express frequent complaints about the low quality of the care given to the adolescents, claiming that the staffing levels were far too low and that the adolescents were not provided with the material means and opportunities to meet their needs. At the administrative meetings of the team, they accused the doctor and the sister in charge of not doing enough to meet those needs; the doctor and the sister in charge then shifted the blame on to the director of the unit, who was accused of failing to respond by making applications to the administration. In fact, the staffing level of the unit was quite satisfactory (and had not changed over the previous year), while living standards were good, too. This was pointed out at planned meetings between the staff and an outside supervisor. After a considerable amount of working out, the therapeutic team of the unit came face-to-face with their fears about violence and aggressiveness. Projection and pres-sure on the doctor, the sister in charge, and the director dwindled and died away, all the staff felt more secure, the aggressiveness of the adolescents was dealt with more effec-tively, and the therapeutic atmosphere of the unit was re-stored.

In other cases, it can happen that the lack of conscience in the young delinquent adolescent with earlier traumatic experi-ences may be the result of the splitting off and projection of a harsh and primitive superego that is unbearable for him. A deprived, inadequately cared for, and traumatized adolescent may project onto the staff an idealized maternal figure and may try to control the staff into behaving in an idealized manner. The risk for both the staff and the adolescents is that the projection may be so compelling that the staff act on it, instead of treating it as a communication. If the staff act under the pressure of coun-tertransference, they may act out the primitive, harsh, projected superego referred to in the first instance and impose an excessively strict and punishing programme. In the second case, they may act out the projected ideal mother and impose a programme that meets every need and makes no attempt to set limits. If the staff are to retain their therapeutic effectiveness, they must restrain themselves from taking action on the basis of their feelings of countertransference, and they must continue to see the traumatized child or adolescent as a disturbed individual in need of help with his disturbed behaviour. If this is not done, both therapist and child or adolescent will merely repeat the past of the child or adolescent rather than making progress on the basis of repeating, remembering, and working through.

In in-patient treatment, there is a tendency for the staff to develop intense phenomena of countertransference stemming from the fact that the child's or adolescent's need for in-patient treatment implies the assumption of a parental role on the part of the staff. This may cause the staff to feel guilty for having substituted themselves for the parents. The staff may keep the guilt at bay through the rationalization that they are the "good" parents who have replaced the "bad" parents. Some of the difficulties that occur between staff and parents are the outcome of the points touched on above, which in turn stem from continuation of the splitting between the parents and the staff of the unit, which is intensified in the treatment of traumatized adolescents. We noted earlier in this chapter (p. 140) that traumatized children and especially adolescents tend, predominantly, to use the mechanisms of denial, splitting, and projective identification. Such adolescents are very sensitive to splitting in others and can utilize this to play one side (e.g. the staff) off against the other (e.g. the parent).

When improvements in the adolescent fail to occur, puzzlement, anxiety, guilt, and helplessness become predominant in the staff, lowering morale and affecting their therapeutic work. In other words, it is as if their fantasy of being good parents has collapsed. In this situation, and as a result of countertransference, the staff may react by ceasing to be "good parents" and becoming aggressive and punitive parents. This then confirms the adolescents' worst fantasies, and they too will become aggressive and violent, leading into a vicious circle of relationships on the unit.

Countertransference reparative actions
and some consequences

It has been reported that children who have undergone abuse (whether physical or emotional) have the initial effect of mobiliz-ing a marked reparative tendency on the part of the members of the staff who are caring for them. Such children or adolescents also display powerful dependency needs, and they become more and more demanding. Indeed, it very often happens that the staff member actually does "give" to such children or adolescents, without limits. However, the moment comes when the child or adolescent becomes violent and aggressive, sometimes literally biting the hand of the carer. These children or adolescent have been described as suffering from traumatic *psychosis* (Strogh, 1974). It goes without saying that the staff member and/or the therapist will feel disillusioned and intensely angry with the child or adolescent, which may affect the therapeutic relationship or even the therapeutic quality of the milieu. To this picture we have to add the dependency needs of the family members, which, when taken together with the frequent crises, will make the staff members feel drained and used. Such a state of affairs may lead to the burn-out syndrome. The staff may also develop intense countertransference reactions, which may affect the therapeutic environment of the unit. Strong reactions of countertransference on the part of the staff may also develop in cases of the in-patient treatment of adolescents who have been traumatized by sexual abuse.

Let me give an example.

An adolescent girl, K

K, an adolescent aged 13 years, was referred to our clinic by colleagues in the paediatric clinic at which she was under treatment for a very serious diabetic condition which had appeared at the age of 3½ (it is, of course, well known that a chronic illness can be experienced as a series of traumatic experiences for a child). During this treatment, she had suf-fered from fainting attacks, which after a thorough medical investigation were judged to be psychological in nature. K also displayed learning difficulties and poor adjustment to school. K was of dubious paternity. Her "lawful" father, with whom the mother had a very poor relationship, died thirteen years ago. Seventeen years ago, the mother had a relationship with the current "step-father", who also suffered from diabetes. K had been badly neglected by her mother and required frequent hospitalization to deal with the comas caused by inadequate administration of her medication. K on admission also made references to a consummated sexual relationship. Tests connected with an infection of her genitals revealed the presence of dead spermatozoa in her vaginal secretions. It seemed highly likely that K had been sexually abused by the step-father. During treatment, K functioned with constant acting out (with depressive feelings alternating with anger and seductive behaviour): for example, she behaved and spoke in such a way as to provoke the boys in the in-patient group, who would then "touch her up" (to use the English equivalent of the Greek term then current in the unit) and addressed her in foul language. As in all abuse cases, intense countertransference phenomena were aroused. Apart from the actual upheaval that K's behaviour caused in the unit, the fact that the upheaval was sexual in nature set off extreme reactions in some of the members of staff, who seemed to be attributing adult sexuality to K. At some point, the suspicion was expressed that K might be pregnant. It was very interesting to note that some members of staff referred with great certainty to anatomical changes in K, such as a swollen abdomen. The staff reached the point of believing that K was pregnant, when in fact she was not. In other words, the countertransference had become so strong in some members of the staff that their perception was impaired. This, of course, created a highly negative climate towards K in the unit, which, in turn, caused her to react with even more severe behaviour disorders, thus completing the vicious circle of relationships.

We should also bear in mind that although countertransference can occur in all cases of the in-patient treatment of children and adolescents, its intensity will depend on the duration of the in-patient treatment of the psychologically traumatized adolescents. It has been observed that lengthy in-patient treatment can cause the adolescent to become the subject of intense staff interest or the reverse (i.e. intense anger). The interest may be associated with rescue fantasies, while the staff may even become aggressive towards a child or adolescent who "resists being saved"—that is, when his symptoms do not improve despite the efforts made by the staff. In cases in which treatment is short-term, the staff can adopt a more disengaged attitude. However, in units in which the adolescents stay for two or three years, the staff become real objects for the residents and the residents become real objects for the staff. This makes it difficult for the staff to maintain an objective attitude (Halperin et al., 1981).

Conclusions

In-patient treatment units for children and adolescents provide fertile ground for the development of a multiplicity of reactions of transference and countertransference, especially with psychologically traumatized children and adolescents. Transference reactions will develop towards the therapist, the staff of the unit, and the unit as an institution, while countertransference develops towards the adolescent, the adolescent's parents, as well as the other members of the staff. It is inherent in the functioning and nature of the therapeutic structure that a degree of splitting should occur, and that the child or adolescent may develop a positive transference towards the therapist, who is idealized as the "good parent", and a negative transference towards the other staff, who become the "bad parents". Similarly, the therapist may develop positive maternal countertransference towards the adolescent, which will reinforce splitting because the adolescent projects all his negative emotions onto the other staff of the unit. Of course, the reverse can also occur when a deprived and traumatized adolescent interprets the therapist's neutrality as an indication of indifference. In such cases, the child or adolescent will regress sharply in his relationship with the staff of the unit, who will become the "good parents" while the therapist is the "bad parent". In both cases, there will be an impairment of the therapeutic effectiveness of the environment, especially when there is a degree of competitiveness between the therapist and the staff. Another phenomenon observed in the in-patient treatment of adolescents—especially of those who are severely deprived and traumatized—is that the adolescents may attempt to re-experience, in the unit, real or fantasy experiences and relationships dating from the time before their admission and directly connected to their problems and previous traumatic experiences. As a result, they severely test the staff and the operating limits of the unit with behaviour that may be highly demanding, destructive, impulsive, seductive, or competitive. Such behavioural patterns, which are related to unresolved conflicts and difficulties in the personality of the children or adolescents, are quite often transferred to, and act upon, relationships amongst the staff, thus interfering with the therapeutic effectiveness of the setting. It is important to remember that, if the staff are to retain their therapeutic effectiveness, they should try to understand the disturbed behaviour of the children or adolescents on the basis of their feelings, and that they should try not to repeat the child's or adolescents' past. This will make it possible for the children/ adolescents to make progress on the basis of repeating, remembering, and working through. This is of the greatest importance if the setting of the unit—represented by the network of relationships among the staff, by the operating limits of the unit, and by its rules—is to provide the traumatized adolescent with a holding environment and function as an adequate mother, giving the adolescent's therapist and the adolescent himself the space and scope to explore the adolescent's conflicts and the roots of his difficulties, fears, and expectations. If this is possible, then the adolescents will be able to discover themselves and discern the continuity in their lives, rather than continuing to repeat traumatic relationships.

REFERENCES

Abend, S. M. (1993). An inquiry into the fate of the transference in psychoanalysis. *Journal of the American Psychoanalytic Association, 41*: 627–651.

Alvarez, A. (1983). Problems in the use of the countertransference: getting it across. *J. Child Psychotherapy, 9*: 7.

Alvarez, A. (1992). *Live Company: Psychoanalytic Psychotherapy with Autistic, Borderline, Deprived and Abused Children.* London: Routledge (Rome: Ubaldini-Astrolabio, 1993; Porto Alegre, Brazil: Artes Medicas, 1994).

Anthony, J. (1986). The contributions of child psychoanalysis to psychoanalysis. *Psychoanalytic Study of the Child, 41*: 61–87.

Anzieu, D. (1973). La bisexualité dans l'auto-analyse de Freud. *Nouvelle Revue de Psychanalyse, 7*: 179–191.

Anzieu, D. (1986). Cadre psychanalytique et enveloppes psychiques. *Journal de la Psychanalyse de l'Enfant, 2*: 12–24.

Aulagnier, P. (1988). Cent fois sur le métier . . . (on remet son écoute). *Topique, 41*: 7–17.

Baudry, F. (1991). The relevance of the analyst's character and attitudes to his work. *Journal of the American Psychoanalytic Association, 39*: 917–938.

Beiser, H. R. (1971). Personality characteristics of child analysts: a comparative study of child analyst students and other students as analysts of adults. *Journal of the American Psychoanalytic Association, 19*: 654–669.

Berlin, I. (1987). Some transference and countertransference issues in the playroom. *Journal of the American Academy of Child and Adolescent Psychiatry, 26* (1): 101–107.

Berman, L. (1949). Countertransference and attitudes of the analyst in the therapeutic process. *Psychiatry, 12*: 159–166.

Bernstein, I. (1957). Panel: indications and goals of child analysis as compared with child psychotherapy. *Journal of the American Psychoanalytic Association, 5*: 158–163.

Bick, E. (1962). Child analysis today. *International Journal of Psycho-Analysis, 43*: 328–332.

Bick, E. (1964). Notes on infant observation in psychoanalytic training. *International Journal of Psycho-Analysis, 45*: 558–560.

Bick, E. (1968). The experience of the skin in early object-relations. *International Journal of Psycho-Analysis, 49*: 484–486.

Bion, W. R. (1962). *Learning from Experience*. London: Heinemann. [Reprinted London: Karnac Books, 1984.]

Bion, W. R. (1963). *Elements of Psycho-Analysis*. London: Heinemann. [Reprinted London: Karnac Books, 1984.]

Bion, W. R. (1965). *Transformations*. London: Heinemann.

Bleger, J. (1967). *Symbiose et ambiguïté*. Paris: PUF, 1981.

Blos, P. (1962). *On Adolescence*. New York: Free Press.

Bower, T. G. R. (1982). *Development in Infancy*. San Francisco, CA: W. H. Freeman.

Brafman, A. (1988). Infant observation. *International Journal of Psycho-Analysis, 15*: 45–61.

Brandell, J. (1992). Countertransference phenomena in the psychotherapy of children and adolescents. In: J. Brandell (Ed.), *Countertransference in Psychotherapy with Children and Adolescents* (pp. 1–46). Northvale, NJ: Jason Aronson.

Brenman-Pick, I. (1985). Working through in the counter-transference. In E. Spillius (Ed.), *Melanie Klein Today, Vol. 2: Mainly Practice*. London: Routledge, 1988.

Britton, R. (1989). Projective identification: communication or evasion? Unpublished paper presented at the British Psycho-Analytic Society.

Cahn, R., & Ladame, F. (1992). Psychothérapie, psychanalyse et adolescence. *Adolescence* [Paris], *10*: 223–235.

Carpy, D. (1989). Tolerating the counter-transference: a mutative process. *International Journal of Psycho-Analysis, 70*: 287–294.

Chessick, R. (1992). What grounds the transference–countertransference interaction? *The American Journal of Psychoanalysis, 52* (4): 327–337.

Coltart, N. (1986). Slouching toward Bethlehem . . . or thinking the unthinkable in psychoanalysis. In: G. Kohon (Ed.), *The British School of Psychoanalysis. The Independent Tradition.* London: Free Association Books.

Diatkine, R., & Simon, J. (1972). *La psychanalyse précoce.* Paris: PUF.

Donnet, J. L. (1973). Le divan bien tempéré. *Nouvelle revue de psychanalyse, 8*: 23–50.

Epstein, L., & Feiner, A. (Eds.) (1983). *Countertransference: The Therapist's Contribution to the Therapeutic Situation.* New York: Jason Aronson.

Fairbairn, W. R. D. (1952). *Psychoanalytic Studies of the Personality.* London: Routledge & Kegan Paul.

Feinsilver, D. (1985). The family meeting as a darkroom: countertransference issues with severely disturbed adolescents. In: S. C. Feinstein (Ed.), *Adolescent Psychiatry, Vol. 12* (pp. 509–523). Chicago, IL: Chicago University Press.

Feldman, M. (1992). Splitting and projective identification. In: R. Anderson (Ed.), *Clinical Lectures on Klein and Bion* (pp. 74–88). London: Tavistock; New York: Routledge.

Fenichel, O. (1945). *The Psychoanalytic Theory of Neurosis.* New York: W. W. Norton.

Fliess, R. (1953). Countertransference and counter-identification. *Journal of the American Psychoanalytic Association, 1*: 268–274.

Freud, S. (1905e). Fragments of an analysis. *S.E., 7*: 3–12.

Freud, S. (1910d). The future prospects of psycho-analytic therapy. *S.E., 11*: 139–151.

Freud, S. (1911c). Psycho-analytic notes on an autobiographical account of a case of paranoia. *S.E., 12.*

Freud, S. (1913i). The disposition to obsessional neurosis. A contribution to the problem of choice of neurosis. *S.E., 12*: 313–326.

Freud, S. (1915a). Observations on transference-love: further recommendations on the technique of psychoanalysis. *S.E.*, *12*: 158–171.

Freud, S. (1915e). The unconscious. *S.E.*, *14*: 161–215.

Freud, S. (1916—17). *Introductory Lectures on Psycho-Analysis. S.E.*, *15 & 16*.

Furst, S. (1986). Psychic trauma and its reconstruction with particular reference to postchildhood trauma. In A. Rothstein (Ed.), *The Reconstruction of Trauma.* Madison, WI: International Universities Press.

Gabel, S., & Bemporad, J. (1994). Variations in countertransference reactions in psychotherapy with children. *American Journal of Psychotherapy, 48* (1): 111.

Gammill, J. (1989). Du contre-transfert de l'analyste envers les parents des enfants en traitement. *Journal de la Psychanalyse de l'Enfant, 6*: 87–119.

Gammill, J. (1992). Introduction to the panel on the questions of frequency in child and adolescent analysis. *Psychoanalysis in Europe, 38*: 97–104.

Garber, B. (1992). Countertransference reactions in death and divorce: comparison and contrast. *Residential Treatment for Children and Youth, 9* (4): 43–60.

Gartner, A. (1985). Countertransference issues in the psychotherapy of adolescents. *Journal of Child and Adolescent Psychotherapy, 2*: 187.

Geltner, P. (1987). Analysis without words: emotional induction in the treatment of a non-expressive child. *Modern Psychoanalysis, 12* (2): 221–230.

Giovacchini, P. (1974). The difficult adolescent patient: countertransference problems. In: S. C. Feinstein (Ed.), *Adolescent Psychiatry, Vol. 3.* New York: Basic Books, 1974.

Giovacchini, P. (1981). Countertransference and the therapeutic turmoil. *Contemporary Psychoanalysis, 17*: 565–594.

Giovacchini, P. (1985). Countertransference and the severely disturbed adolescent. In: S. C. Feinstein (Ed.), *Adolescent Psychiatry, Vol. 12.* Chicago, IL: University of Chicago Press.

Glover, E. (1955). *The Technique of Psychoanalysis.* London: Hogarth Press.

Gochman, E. R. G. (1992). On countertransference. *International Journal of Psycho-Analysis, 1*: 81–84.

Godfrind, J. (1993). *Les deux courants du transfert*. Paris: PUF.

Grinberg, L. (1979). Projective counteridentification and counter-transference. In: L. Epstein & A. Feiner (Eds.), *Countertransference: The Therapist's Contribution to the Therapeutic Situation*. Northvale, NJ: Jason Aronson.

Grotstein, J. S. (1981). Wilfred R. Bion: the man, the psychoanalyst, the mystic. A perspective on his life and work. In: *Do I Dare Disturb the Universe?* Beverly Hills, CA: Caesura Press.

Grotstein, J. (1985). Splitting and projective identification in psycho-analytic therapy. In: *Splitting and Projective Identification*. New York: Jason Aronson.

Greenacre, P. (1954). The role of transference. *Journal of the American Psychoanalytical Association, 2*: 671–684.

Haag, G. (1983). Racines précocissimes de la détermination sexuelle ou la bisexualité dans la relation orale. *Les textes du Centre Alfred Binet, 2*: 69–72.

Haag, G. (1985). La mère et le bébé dans les deux moitiés du corps. *Neuropsychiatrie de l'Enfance et de l'Adolescence, 33* (2–3): 107–114.

Halperin, D., Laura, G., Miscione, F., Rebhan, J., Schnabelk, J., & Shachter, B. (1981). Countertransference issues in a transitional residential treatment program for troubled adolescents. In: S. C. Feinstein (Ed.), *Adolescent Psychiatry, Vol. 9*. Chicago, IL: University of Chicago Press.

Hammer, M., & Kaplan, A. (1967). Theoretical considerations in the practice of psychotherapy with children. In: M. Hammer & A. Kaplan (Eds.), *The Practice of Psychotherapy with Children* (pp. 27–38). Homewood, IL: Dorsey Press.

Heimann, P. (1950). On countertransference. *International Journal of Psychoanalysis, 31*: 81–84.

Heimann, P. (1960). Counter-transference. *British Journal of Medical Psychology, 33*: 9–15.

Hinshelwood, R. D. (1989). *A Dictionary of Kleinian Thought*. London: Free Association Books.

Holder, A. (1991). Kinderanalyse und analytische Kindertherapie. *Zeitschrift für psychoanalytische Theorie und Praxis, 6*: 407–419.

James, O. (1987). *The Role of the Nurse Therapist Relationship in the Therapeutic Community* (pp. 78–94), ed. R. Kennedy, A. Heymans, & L. Tishler. London: Free Association Books.

Joseph, B. (1988). Projective identification: clinical aspects. In: J. Sandler (Ed.), *Projection, Identification, Projective Identification*. London: Karnac Books.

Joseph, B. (1989). *Psychic Equilibrium and Psychic Change*, ed. M. Feldman & E. Bott-Spillius. London: Tavistock; New York: Routledge. [Reprinted London: Karnac Books, 1993.]

Kernberg, O. (1965). Notes on countertransference. *Journal of the American Psychoanalytic Association, 13*: 38–56.

Kernberg, O. (1988). Projection and projective identification: developmental and clinical aspects. In: J. Sandler (Ed.), *Projection, Identification, Projective Identification*. London: Karnac Books.

King, C. (1976). Countertransference and counter-experience in the treatment of violence-prone youth. *American Journal of Orthopsychiatry, 46* (1): 43.

King, P. (1978). Affective response of the analyst to the patients' communications. *International Journal of Psycho-Analysis, 59*: 329–335.

Klein, M. (1937). Love, guilt and reparation. In: *Love, Guilt and Reparation and Other Works 1921–1945*. London: Hogarth Press & The Institute of Psycho-Analysis, 1975.

Klein, M. (1946). Notes on some schizoid mechanisms. In: *Envy and Gratitude and Other Works 1946–1963*. London: Hogarth Press and The Institute of Psycho-Analysis, 1975.

Klein, M. (1957). Envy and gratitude. In: *Envy and Gratitude and Others Works 1946–1963*. London, Hogarth Press and The Institute of Psycho-Analysis, 1975.

Kohut, H. (1971). *Analysis of the Self: A Systematic Approach to the Psychoanalytic Treatment of Narcissistic Personality Disorders*. New York: International Universities Press.

Kohrman, R., Fineberg, H., Gelman, R., & Weiss, S. (1971). Technique of child analysis: problems of countertransference. *International Journal of Psycho-Analysis, 52*: 487.

Kris, E. (1978). The recovery of childhood memories in psychoanalysis. *The Psychoanalytic Study of the Child, 33:* 81–116. New Haven, CT: Yale University Press.

Lacan, J. (1966). *Ecrits*. Paris: Seuil [English translation: *Ecrits: A Selection*. London: Hogarth Press, 1977.]

Ladame, F. (1995). The importance of dream and action in the adolescent process. *International Journal of Psycho-Analysis, 76*: 1143–1154.

Langs, J. (1979). *The Therapeutic Environment*. New York: Aronson.

Laplanche, J. (1992). Du transfert: sa provocation par l'analyste. *Psychanalyse à l'Université*, 17: 3–22.

Laplanche, J., & Pontalis, J. B. (1973). *The Language of Psychoanalysis*. London: Hogarth Press. [Reprinted London: Karnac Books, 1988.]

Laufer, M., & Laufer, E. (Eds.) (1989). *Developmental Breakdown and Psychoanalytic Treatment in Adolescence. Clinical Studies*. New Haven, CT: Yale University Press.

Little, M. (1951). Countertransference and the patient's response to it. *International Journal of Psycho-Analysis*, 32: 32–40.

Malmquist, C. P. (1978). *Handbook of Adolescence*. New York: Aronson.

Marcus, I. (1980). Countertransference and the psychoanalytic process in children and adolescents. *Psychoanalytic Study of the Child*, 35: 285–299.

Marshall, R. (1983). Countertransference with children and adolescents. In: L. Epstein & A. H. Feiner (Eds.), *Countertransference: The Therapist's Contribution to the Therapeutic Situation* (pp. 407–444). New York: Jason Aronson.

McCarthy, J. (1989). Resistance and countertransference in child and adolescent psychotherapy. *The American Journal of Psychoanalysis*, 49 (1): 67–76.

Meissner, W. (1987). Adolescent paranoia: transference and countertransference issues. In: S. C. Feinstein (Ed.), *Adolescent Psychiatry, Vol. 12*. Chicago, IL: University of Chicago Press.

Meltzer, D. (1966). The relation of anal masturbation to projective identification. *International Journal of Psycho-Analysis*, 47: 56–67.

Meltzer, D., Bremner, J., Hoxter, S., Weddell, D., & Wittenberg, I. (1975). *Explorations in Autism*. London: Clunie Press.

Menzies Lyth, I. (1985). The development of the self in children in institutions. *Journal of Child Psychotherapy*, 11: 49–64.

Miller, L., Rustin, M., & Shuttleworth, J. (1989). *Closely Observed Infants*. London: Duckworth.

Muir, B. (1987). Is inpatient psychotherapy a valid concept? In: R. Kennedy, A. Heymans, & L. Tishler (Eds.), *The Family as Inpatient* (pp. 64–77). London: Free Association Books.

Norman, J. (1993). Frequency in child and adolescent analysis. *Psychoanalysis in Europe*, 41: 60–64.

Orr, D. W. (1954). Transference and Countertransference. *Journal of the American Psychoanalytical Association, 2*: 621–670.

Palombo, J. (1985): Self-psychology and countertransference in the treatment of children. *Child and Adolescent Social Work, 2* (1): 36.

Papousek, H., & Papousek, M. (1976). Mothering and the cognitive head start: psychobiological considerations. In: H. R. Schaffer (Ed.), *Studies in Mother–Infant Interaction.* London: Academic Press.

Piene, F., Auestad, A., Lange, J., & Leira, T. (1983). Countertransference–transference seen from the point of view of child psychoanalysis. *Scandinavian Psychoanal., Rev., 6*: 43–57.

Racker, H. (1968). *Transference and countertransference.* London: Karnac Books, 1985.

Rayner, E. (1981). Infant experiences, affects and the characteristics of the unconscious. *International Journal of Psycho-Analysis, 62*: 403–412.

Reich, A. (1966). Further remarks on countertransference. *International Journal of Psychoanalysis, 32*: 25–31.

Rosenfeld, H. (1965). *Psychotic States. A Psychoanalytical Approach.* London: Hogarth Press.

Rosenfeld, H. (1969). Contribution to the psychopathology of psychotic states: the importance of projective identification in the ego structure and object relations of the psychotic patient. In: P. Doucet & C. Laurin (Eds.), *Problems of Psychosis.* The Hague: Excerpta Medica.

Rosenfeld, H. (1987). The influence of projective identification on the analyst's task. In: *Impasse and Interpretation* (pp. 157–264). London: Tavistock.

Sandler, J. (1987). Countertransference and role-responsiveness. In: Edmond Slakter (Ed.), *Countertransference.* New York: Jason Aronson.

Sandler, J. (1988). *Projection, Identification, Projective Identification.* London: Karnac Books.

Sandler, J., Kennedy, H., & Tyson, R. L. (1980). *The Technique of Child Psychoanalysis.* London: Hogarth Press.

Schowalter, J. (1985). Countertransference in work with children: review of a neglected concept. *Journal of the American Academy of Child Psychiatry, 25* (1): 40.

Shane, M. (1980). Countertransference and the developmental orientation and approach. *Psychoanalysis and Contemporary Thought, 3*: 195–212.

Spillius, E. B. (1983). Developments from the work of Melanie Klein. *International Journal of Psycho-Analysis, 64* (3).

Spillius, E. B. (1992). Clinical experiences of projective identification. In: *Clinical Lectures on Klein and Bion*. London: Routledge/New Library in Psychoanalysis.

Spitz, R. A. (1946). Anaclitic depression. *Psychoanalytic Study of the Child, 2*: 313–342.

Steiner, R. (1994). Some observations on the role played by extra-analytical variables in the theoretical and clinical issues of the Freud–Klein Controversial Discussions, 1941–44, and their relevance today. *Festschrift*, Professor Joseph Sandler.

Strogh, G. (1974). Psychotic children. In: Ph. Baker (Ed.), *The Residential Psychiatric Treatment of Children* (pp. 178–204). London: Crosby Lockwood Staples.

Sullivan, H. S. (1953). *The Interpersonal Theory of Psychiatry*. New York: W. W. Norton.

Symington, N. (1986). The analyst's act of freedom as agent of therapeutic change. In G. Kohon (Ed.), *The British School of Psychoanalysis. The Independent Tradition*. London: Free Association Books.

Temeles, P. (1967). Gift-giving. *Bulletin of the Philadelphia Association of Psychoanal, 17*: 31–32.

Tower, L. (1956). Countertransference. *Journal of the American Psychoanalytic Association, 4*: 224–255.

Trevarthen, C. (1978). Modes of perceiving and codes of acting. In: H. J. Pick (Ed.), *Psychological Modes of Perceiving and Processing Information*. Hillsdale, NJ: Lawrence Erlbaum.

Trowell, J., & Miles, G. (1991). The contribution of observation training to professional development in social work. *Journal of Social Work Practice, 8* (1): 51–60.

Trowell, J., & Rustin, M. (1991). Developing the internal observer in professionals in training. *Infant Mental Health, 12* (3): 233–245.

Tustin, F. (1981). *Autistic States in Children*. London: Routledge & Kegan Paul (2nd ed. 1992).

Tyson, P. (1980). The gender of the analyst, in relation to transference and countertransference manifestations in pre-latency children. *Psychanalytic Study of the Child, 35*: 321–338.

Waksman, J. (1986). The countertransference of the child analyst. *International Review of Psycho-Analysis, 13*: 405.

Wallace, N., & Wallace, M. E. (1985). Transference/countertransference issues in the treatment of an acting-out adolescent. In S. C. Feinstein (Ed.), *Adolescent Psychiatry, Vol. 12*. Chicago, IL: University of Chicago Press.

Wiesse, J., & Kroczek-Weinstock, E. (1989). Anxiety in adolescence and its significance for psychoanalysis. *Adolescence, 24* (94): 403.

Winnicott, D. W. (1947). Hate in the counter-transference. In: *Through Paediatrics to Psychoanalysis* (pp. 194–203). London: Hogarth Press, 1975. [Reprinted London: Karnac Books, 1992.]

Winnicott, D. W. (1965). *The Maturational Processes and the Facilitating Environment: Studies in the Theory of Emotional Development*. London: Hogarth Press; New York: International Universities Press. [Reprinted London: Karnac Books, 1990.]

Winnicott, D. W. (1971). *Therapeutic Consultations in Child Psychiatry*. London: Hogarth Press.

Woolridge, M. W. (1986). The "anatomy"of infant sucking. *Midwifery, 2* (4): 164–171.

Zaslow, S. (1985). Countertransference issues in psychotherapy with adolescents. In: S. C. Feinstein (Ed.), *Adolescent Psychiatry, Vol. 12*. Chicago, IL: University of Chicago Press.

Zinner, J., & Shapiro, R. (1972). Projective identification as a mode of perception and behaviour in families of adolescents. *International Journal of Psycho-Analysis, 53*: 523–530.

INDEX